BATMAN™ AND THE JOKER™

BEST OF ENEMIES

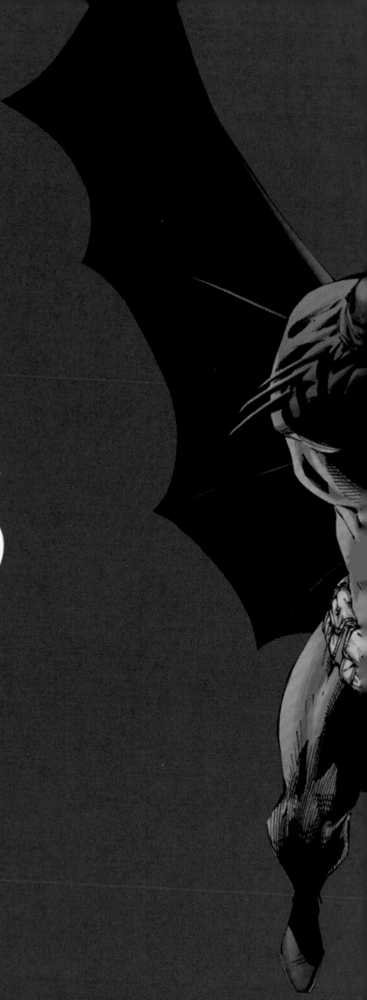

CONTENTS

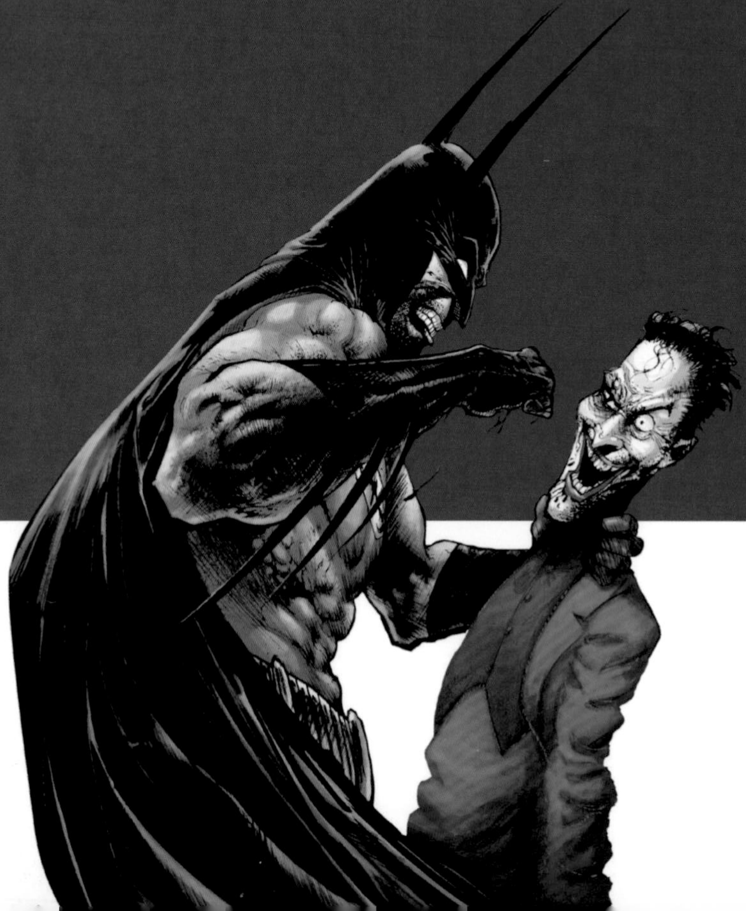

ETERNAL ENEMIES

Batman and The Joker – two eternal opposites, the savior
of Gotham City and its tormentor. One seeks to protect the
innocent, the other wants to prove to them that life is all one
sick joke. Batman believes in the good in all of us. Clown
Prince of Crime believes we are all just one bad day away
from being as mad as he is.

This book explores a rivalry that goes back to Batman #1
(Spring 1940) and is still as compelling as ever, revealing
something of heroism and madness that lurks in our own souls.
This guide celebrates the greatest tales from over seventy-five
years of conflict, including the stories of Grant Morrison
and Scott Snyder. Spectacular visuals include the work of
Frank Miller and Greg Capullo.

This essential companion also takes you behind the scenes to
discover the secrets of the world of Gotham City, from the
Batcave to the Gotham City Police Department files on The
Joker. Taking you right up to the present day, these pages
will help you decide who really has the last laugh …

BATMAN

Batman is a true icon. From his first appearance in *Detective Comics* through to his big screen outings, the Dark Knight has

RISE OF THE DARK KNIGHT

HE'S THE DARK KNIGHT DETECTIVE. GOTHAM'S GUARDIAN AND ONE OF THE GREATEST HEROES OF ALL TIME. WE REVEAL THE HISTORY OF THE DARK KNIGHT PRE-DC COMICS: NEW 52...

When Bruce Wayne's parents were gunned down, the young Bruce made an oath to rid the world of the criminal scourge that had killed them. To this end he turned to the martial arts and travelled the world to perfect himself. Training under great masters, Bruce honed his skills for more than a decade, until he was the most accomplished martial artist in the world. On his travels he also studied various mental disciplines at the world's most prestigious universities, molding his mind as well as his body. By the time he returned to Gotham City, he had become a Renaissance man, with an intellect rivalled only by the likes of business magnate Lex Luthor. At long last Bruce Wayne could fulfil his oath and begin his mission.

NIGHT OF THE BAT

He soon found out that Gotham City's streets didn't welcome heroes. Shot, beaten, and close to death, Bruce's first night trying to bring justice to Gotham City was almost his last. Recovering from his injuries, Bruce realized he needed more than brains and brawn to battle injustice – he needed something to strike real fear into a villain's heart.

Fate intervened, when a lone bat smashed its way into his study and Bruce recalled a childhood experience when he'd been terrified by the bats living in the caverns underneath the family estate.

WELL, DICK, NOW THAT YOUR PARENTS' DEATHS HAVE BEEN AVENGED, ARE YOU GOING BACK TO CIRCUS LIFE?

NO, I THINK MOTHER AND DAD WOULD LIKE ME TO GO ON FIGHTING CRIME,—AND AS FOR ME...WELL... I LOVE ADVENTURE!

Dynamic duo. Robin is a loyal sidekick, foil and companion.

How, father? How do I do it?

If I ring this bell, Alfred will come.

He can stop the bleeding, in time.

Another of your gifts to me, father.

I have wealth. The family manor rests above a huge cave that will be the perfect headquarters...

What do I use... to make them afraid?

...even a butler with training in combat medic..

Blood oath. Bruce Wayne swears revenge on the criminals who prey on the weak.

Grim responsibility. Batman holds the lifeless body of Jason Todd in his hands.

He took the image of the bat and turned it into a dark and menacing costume. The bat would now become an emblem of terror for the countless thugs and criminals of Gotham City. Bruce Wayne fought his war alone in the beginning, but fate ensured that he would eventually have comrades to assist him in his struggle.

THE BOY WONDER

Dick Grayson was a young circus acrobat who witnessed his family being murdered by the mob, victims of a protection racket. Bruce Wayne took the boy in and trained Dick to become a costumed crime fighter, giving him

the name Robin. Grayson excelled at fighting the forces of evil, and his cocky smile and clever circus tricks brought a lighter mood to the grim business of keeping Gotham City safe. Some believe the young hero even prevented Batman from going too far down his own dark road.

Dick Grayson eventually decided to step outside of Batman's shadow. After a few years fighting as part of the Teen Titans, he changed his name to Nightwing and moved to the nearby city of Blüdhaven. In time, others would inherit the role of Robin.

The first was troubled teenager Jason Todd. Filled with anger, Jason often refused to listen to his mentor and took chances. Eventually, the Joker killed him. After Jason's tragic death, Batman didn't want to place another teenager in danger as his sidekick. But he hadn't counted on the persistence of the young Tim Drake. Tim used his detective skills to work out who Batman really was, and pestered the unwilling Dark Knight until he was finally allowed to prove himself in the role of Robin. It was a role Tim made his own.

BREAKING THE BAT
One of Batman's darkest moments came at the hands of Bane. This ferocious criminal had been raised in the vicious Santa Prisca prison of Peña Dura. Bane struggled to survive among his fellow inmates but became a ferocious fighter and criminal mastermind. A drug called venom boosted his strength to superhuman levels. Escaping jail, he made his way to Gotham City with one goal in mind: to destroy the Dark Knight.

The first step in his plot was to release all of the villains in Arkham Asylum. Bane watched from afar as Batman battled to recapture the plague of villains. Batman took every single one of his released rogues down and made it back home, battered, bruised and exhausted, only to find Bane waiting for him. Bane not only defeated Batman but, as a *coup de grace*, shattered his spine and threw him onto the Gotham City streets, bleeding and broken.

THE 'NEW' BATMAN
Before Bane's attack, Wayne had acquired an apprentice, Jean-Paul Valley. He now bestowed on him both his costume and his mission, while he himself travelled to the other side of the world to recover. Eventually restored to health, Bruce had to take back his costume and identity by force from an increasingly fanatical apprentice.

CATACLYSM
Batman returned to take back the night, but he was to discover that he could not fight the inherent evils of politics. In an event of Biblical proportions, plague ravaged Gotham City – which was then struck by a cataclysmic earthquake. This double blow decimated the city. Despite valiant attempts by Bruce Wayne to obtain aid, the US

government decided the whole urban area was beyond salvation. It gave residents a warning: get out or be trapped in the city – which was now designated an unrecoverable No Man's Land.

The bridges leading out of the city were destroyed, and the citizens left behind were at the mercy of the super-villains who rose to rule the ruins. But street by street, block by block, Batman, Commissioner James Gordon, and other heroes fought back the wave of villainy and eventually regained control of the city. Seizing an opportunity, Lex Luthor swept into Gotham City with aid, supplies, and funding. He used cash to get credit and prestige for saving Gotham City and earned enough political capital to become the new US president.

WANTED
Bruce now found himself accused of the murder of his ex-girlfriend, Vesper Fairchild. Finding himself at the scene of the crime with a gun in his hand, Bruce fled and went underground while trying to clear his name. Through detective work, Batman revealed the true culprit and cleared the name of his alter ego. The murderer turned out to be President Lex Luthor, who had committed the crime in an attempt to smear his billionaire rival's name. Batman, with some help from Superman, brought Luthor to justice.

Bane strikes. **The insane villain breaks the Dark Knight's back.**

THE BATCAVE

Private viewing. **The trophy room in the new Batcave.**

The original Batcave was situated under Wayne Manor and was destroyed in the earthquake that devastated Gotham City. The new base is also under Wayne Manor but makes more use of the cave's height. Spread over eight levels, the new cave contains space for Batman's various vehicles, including his extensive collection of Batmobiles, while also providing state-of-the-art medical and training facilities. At the centre of the cave is Batman's advanced computer system. Powered by seven Cray T392 mainframes, and including a holographic projector, the new system gives Bruce quicker access to his massive crime file database than ever before. High-speed internet links ensure this is kept fully up to date. The cave's power is provided by multiple hydrogen generators. Batman also has a number of smaller caves scattered across the world for use in emergencies. One of these is positioned under Arkham Asylum, and another is under the Robinson Park reservoir in Gotham City.

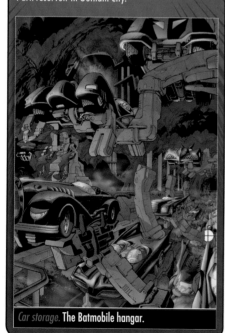

Car storage. **The Batmobile hangar.**

He's immensely powerful—

Evil angel. **Batman comes into conflict with the vicious Azrael.**

HUSH

Bruce found himself at the center of another attack when his childhood friend, Dr. Thomas Elliot, returned to Gotham City. It seemed Elliot had come back to save an injured Batman with his surgical skills, but in reality he was a criminal mastermind known as Hush. With the help of the Riddler, he orchestrated a number of attacks on the Dark Knight. At one point, it appeared Hush had used the supervillain Clayface to make it look like Jason Todd had returned from the dead.

Only later did Batman learn the shocking truth: Todd had returned, thanks to a reality-changing wave caused by the evil Superboy Prime punching his way through reality.

THE JUSTICE LEAGUE OF AMERICA

Batman has teamed up with many costumed allies, even helping to create the world's

I KNOW WHAT YOU'RE PLANNING.

THIS IS MY CITY.

FOR NOW.

Political animal. **Batman warns Luthor to leave Gotham City alone.**

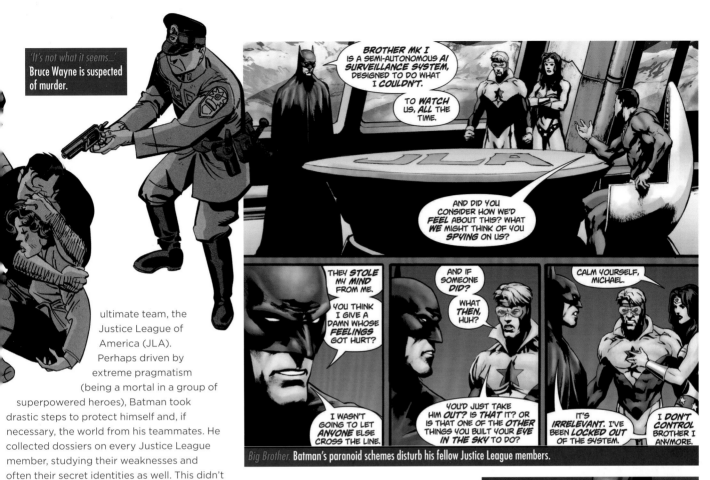

'It's not what it seems...' Bruce Wayne is suspected of murder.

ultimate team, the Justice League of America (JLA). Perhaps driven by extreme pragmatism (being a mortal in a group of superpowered heroes), Batman took drastic steps to protect himself and, if necessary, the world from his teammates. He collected dossiers on every Justice League member, studying their weaknesses and often their secret identities as well. This didn't go over well with the League, and Batman was asked to leave. His paranoia was justified, however, as he discovered League member Zatanna had once modified his memory in the recent past.

BROTHER EYE
The Brother Eye satellite was a sophisticated piece of technology that Batman designed to combat a potential world of superheroes gone mad. It evolved a mind of its own and unleashed OMAC (Observational Meta-Human Activity Construct) units to do the bidding of Maxwell Lord, leader of the government organization known as Checkmate. These "units," actually human beings taken over by cybernetics, aided another attempt by Lex Luthor to take over the world. Lord was eventually defeated,

Political animal. Batman warns Luthor to leave Gotham City alone.

and Batman, with the help of his JLA teammates, destroyed the satellite and bested Luthor. Concerned that fear and distrust were leading him away from the path of justice, Batman departed to consider his future, leaving the reformed supervillain, Harvey Dent, to watch over his city.

SON OF THE DEMON
On his return home a year later, Batman encountered Talia Head, the daughter of immortal villain Ra's al Ghul. He learned that, years before, he had unknowingly fathered a son called Damian with her. Talia had hidden the child away, training him to become a killer. Bruce took on Damian, trying to adjust to his new role of father. For his part, Damian was jealous of those close to his father and tried to prove himself the only way he could: by viciously beating Robin and taking his place. While Bruce came to care for his son, they were torn apart when Bruce was attacked by Doctor Simon Hurt, and then Darkseid.

Hurt was a criminal mastermind and leader of the Black Glove, a deadly criminal group. He took Batman's life apart piece by piece, leaving Batman drugged out and confused, wandering Gotham City's streets hallucinating strange creatures. One of these hallucinations took the form of Bat-Mite, and

Big Brother. Batman's paranoid schemes disturb his fellow Justice League members.

Checkmate. The Bat in the crushing grip of an OMAC.

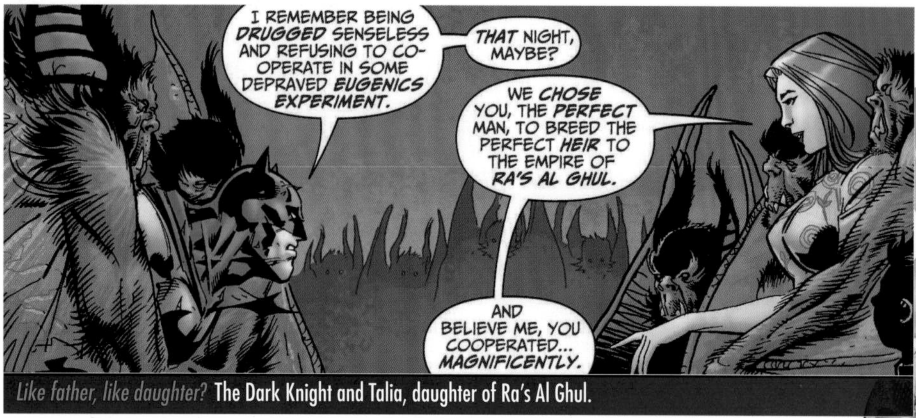
I REMEMBER BEING DRUGGED SENSELESS AND REFUSING TO CO-OPERATE IN SOME DEPRAVED EUGENICS EXPERIMENT.
THAT NIGHT, MAYBE?
WE CHOSE YOU, THE PERFECT MAN, TO BREED THE PERFECT HEIR TO THE EMPIRE OF RA'S AL GHUL.
AND BELIEVE ME, YOU COOPERATED... MAGNIFICENTLY.

Like father, like daughter? **The Dark Knight and Talia, daughter of Ra's Al Ghul.**

was part of a psychological failsafe Bruce had installed in his brain to deal with such attacks. Some believed Hurt to be the devil. Hurt himself claimed to be Bruce's father, Thomas Wayne, and that he had arranged his wife's shooting to rid himself of her. Batman and Hurt had a ferocious showdown that resulted in Hurt's helicopter exploding, leaving him presumed dead.

DARKSEID STRIKES

When the new God Orion was found dead, Batman was called on to investigate. He was captured by Darkseid, who sought to unleash the Anti-Life equation in order to reshape reality in his own twisted image. Batman managed to stop his plans, shooting the villain with the same bullet that had been used to murder Orion. At the same time Darkseid blasted Batman with his Omega Beams, seemingly killing the Dark Knight.

BATMAN REBORN

With Batman gone, a battle for his cowl occurred as several of his allies sought to inherit the role. In the end it was Dick Grayson who did so, forming a strong bond with Damian Wayne who became the new Robin. Only Tim Drake refused to acknowledge that their mentor was truly dead, and eventually managed to prove that Batman was indeed alive – but lost in time. Darkseid had turned Batman into a living weapon, and as the Dark Knight was being

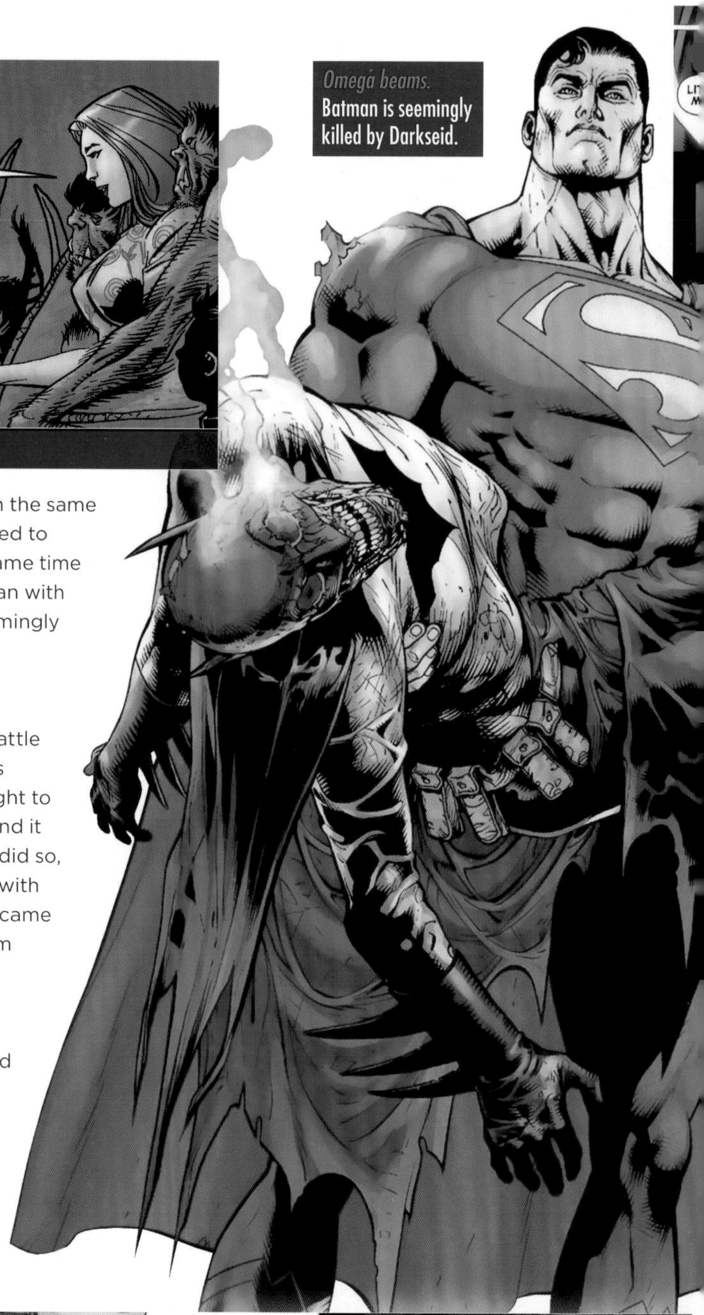

Omega beams. **Batman is seemingly killed by Darkseid.**

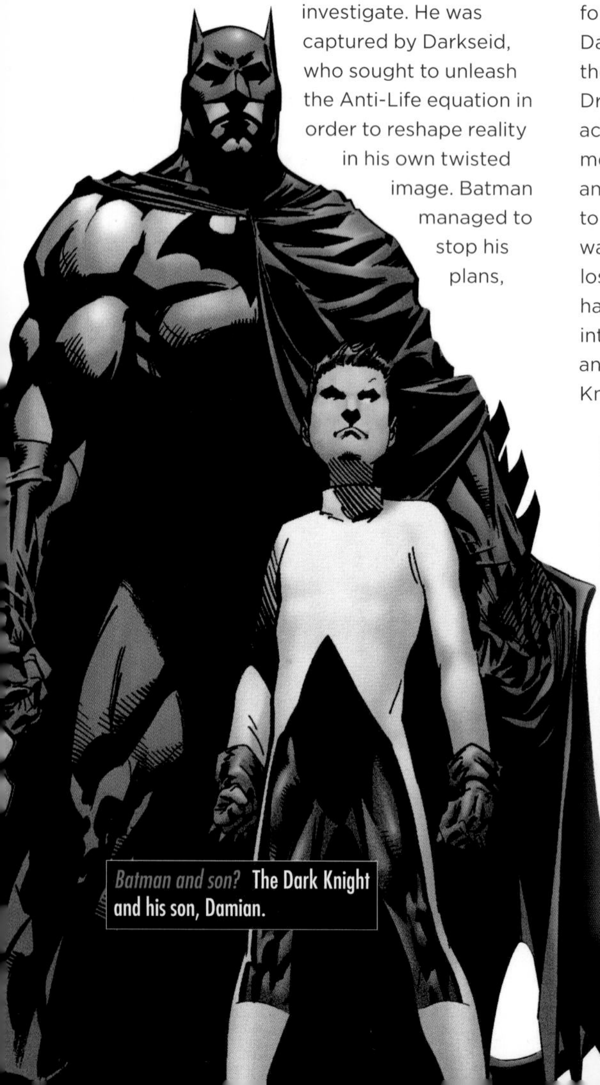

Batman and son? **The Dark Knight and his son, Damian.**

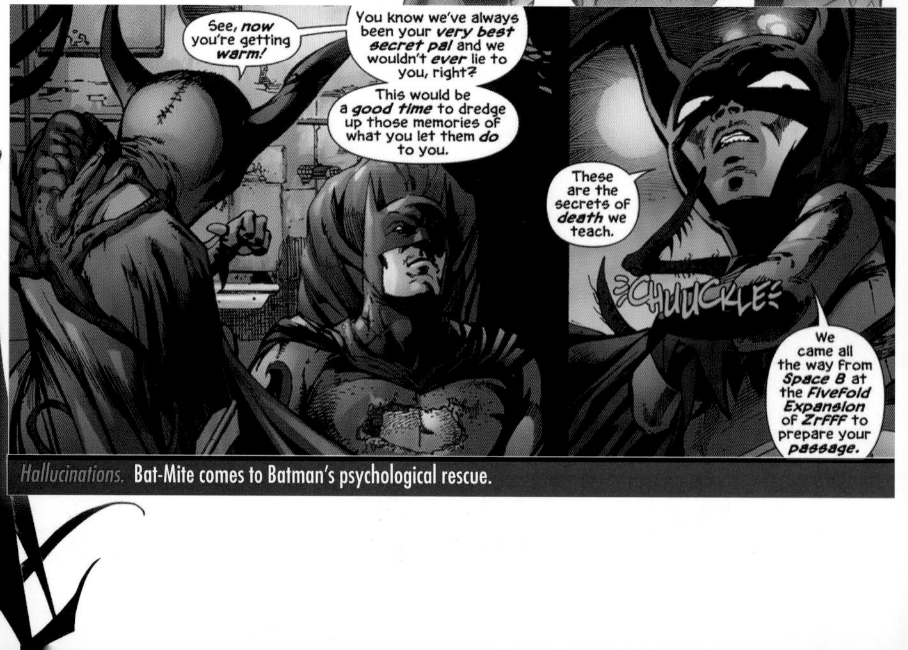
See, now you're getting warm!
You know we've always been your very best secret pal and we wouldn't ever lie to you, right?
This would be a good time to dredge up those memories of what you let them do to you.
These are the secrets of death we teach.
CHUCKLE
We came all the way from Space B at the Fivefold Expansion of Zrfff to prepare your passage.

Hallucinations. **Bat-Mite comes to Batman's psychological rescue.**

Batman Inc. Crime fighters united.

been gunned down with his mother and Thomas Wayne had survived to become Batman. But the Flash altered reality again, so that Bruce Wayne was again Batman, but with some of his history changed. It was the start of a dangerous new era for the Dark Knight (See Ascendence of the Bat, page 12).

pulled through time back to the present, his body was building up energy that would destroy the world when he reached the present. Fortunately, Batman's allies came to his aid and freed him of the deadly energy.

Batman returned to Gotham City with a belief that it was not just Gotham City that needed his help. He created Batman Inc., an organization for establishing other heroes as Batman-style crime fighters across the globe. However, reality itself was changed when superhero the Flash travelled back in time, altering history. In this new reality, Bruce Wayne had

New team. Dick Grayson and Damian Wayne.

ETERNAL WAR

A complex plot to destroy Batman was launched by a mysterious figure who appeared to know everything about him. The plan used previous foes like crime boss Carmine Falcone and Hush to torment Batman, and included framing and imprisoning James Gordon. Despite the revelation that Lincoln March was behind the plan, doubt remained as to whether March could be Bruce's long-lost brother. Despite Batman's beaten state, all his allies and supporters in the city rose up to take his part and prove that Batman was more than just one man: he was a spirit of resistance.

Batman became a mentor to two new young heroes, Gotham (Henry Clover Jnr) and Gotham Girl (Claire Clover), who had superpowers tied in to their life-force. But the new heroes were targeted by the mind-corrupting influence of Psycho-Pirate, working for old enemy Hugo Strange. With the JLA, Batman overcame Gotham, who perished from the over-use of his powers.

SUICIDE MISSION

Psycho-Pirate had left Gotham Girl broken and Batman resolved to help her. Psycho-Pirate fled to the Caribbean island of Santa Prisca, under the protection of Bane. Batman assembled a team of villains from Arkham – including his old ally Catwoman – to conduct a 'suicide' mission to capture Psycho-Pirate. The mission succeeded, although Batman barely survived a revenge trip to Gotham by Bane himself.

Batman had kept Psycho-Pirate's mask, and this had strange consequences. It reacted with an enigmatic smiley button in the wall of the Batcave, which caused Batman to take a trip through time. Travelling with the Flash, Batman visited a timeline previously created by the speedster when he had attempted to save the life of his mother. In this timeline, Batman met his true father, Thomas Wayne, who advised Bruce to give up his war and find happiness. Bruce's proposal to Selina Kyle ushered in the dramatic prospect of a wedding... between Batman and Catwoman.

ASCENDENCE OF THE BAT

THE EVENTS OF FLASHPOINT ALTERED THE ENTIRE DC COMICS UNIVERSE. WE EXPLORE THE DARK KNIGHT'S UPDATED PAST AND HIS LATEST ADVENTURES...

> WHAT DONE? I DRESSED THE F OR RATHER, UNDRESSED THEM OFF THE CLOTHES THAT INVISIBLE TO EVERYO YOU, MY KINE
>
> EXPOOOOOO THEM.
>
> AND SPEAKING EXPOSING, MR. PENN WOULD YOU SERV PLEASSSSSSSS

> IT MUST HAVE BEEN THE *WORST DAY* OF YOUR LIFE, THE DAY THEY DIED.

> WELL, I MEAN, BESIDES *TODAY*, OF COURSE. I'M SURE THIS'LL SHOCK YOU, BRUCE-- BUT THE TRUTH IS, IT CHANGED *MY LIFE*, TOO--YOUR PARENTS' DEATHS. CHANGED MY LIFE *FOREVER*.

Beaten. Bruce is nearly killed by the Red Hood Gang.

Chemical demise. The Red Hood Gang leader falls.

Post Flashpoint, the events of Bruce Wayne's past changed slightly. After travelling the world to train, the young Bruce had returned to Gotham City in secret, fighting crime from the shadows, using various disguises to do so. At the time the Red Hood Gang was running riot through the city and had even infiltrated the police and big business. Bruce was aided by the ever-loyal Alfred but nearly killed during an early run in with the gang (after they were tipped off from the Riddler). While recovering from his injuries in his father's study Bruce asked his father for guidance. When a bat flew into the study, his course was set. In his new guise as Batman, Bruce took on the Red Hood Gang, stopping their plan to use toxins from an ACE Chemical plant against the city. The leader of the Red Hood Gang fell to his apparent death in a vat of chemicals during a final confrontation with Batman. While the Red Hood Gang was defeated, Riddler was soon reveled as the real threat to Gotham City. The villain not only defeated Batman but took over Gotham City, creating a "Zero Year" where everything was under his control. Batman had nearly died trying to stop Riddler's plans but after recovering returned to save Gotham City from the madman.

POWERFUL ENEMIES

When Darkseid threatened Earth, Batman joined forces with Superman, Wonder Woman, Green Lantern, Cyborg and Flash to form the Justice League. As part of the League, Batman fought various threats – including an attack from the Crime Syndicate, a twisted version of the Justice League from a parallel Earth.

In time secrets from Gotham City's past were revealed. The greatest was the Court of Owls, a secret cabal that had been controlling Gotham City for decades. When Bruce Wayne declared his plans to make a better Gotham, it brought him to the Court's attention. They sent one of their deadly agents – known as a Talon – to kill him, Bruce just surviving the encounter. The Court then unleashed all their Talons on the city's brightest and best – including Bruce Wayne. While Bruce

Macabre game. Joker taunts the Bat-family.

Casuality of war. Robin is killed fighting Leviathan.

Power of life. Damian Wayne is resurrected.

fought them in the Batcave, his allies tried to protect their would-be victims across the city. Lincoln March, one of Bruce's new friends, was seemingly killed by a Talon but managed to give Batman the names of three members of the Court of Owls.

After tracking the Court of Owls to their base, Batman was surprised to find them all dead at a dining table. Batman then realised it was actually Lincoln March who had been manipulating events. March had faked his own death using technology created by the Court to reanimate Talons. He also claimed to be Bruce Wayne's younger brother, telling Batman that Thomas and Martha Wayne had institutionalized him when he'd been hurt in a car accident as a baby. Batman and March had one final battle across Gotham, March apparently dying when a building exploded, although his body was never found.

FAMILY ISSUES

The Joker remained Batman's greatest foe. During one attack on the Dark Knight and his allies, he captured the Bat-family and made them believe he had sliced the skin off their faces and was trying to feed their skin to them. In reality he had just covered their faces in blood soaked bandages. Batman managed to escape but his allies were sprayed with Joker Toxin. At the end of the fight between Batman and his enemy, the Joker fell to his death – at least so it seemed. Batman's allies recovered but the experience left them all shaken and they distanced themselves from their mentor for a while.

DEATH IN THE FAMILY

Soon after, tragedy struck when Damian was killed during Batman's war with Leviathan. This led to a final showdown between Talia and the Dark Knight, one that ended with Kathy Kane, a spy in Talia's organization, shooting her. Kane worked for a spy group called Spyral, and had made a deal to help Batman against Leviathan as long as the Dark Knight disbanded Batman Incorporated following Leviathan's destruction. After their pyric victory, Batman did just that. Batman Incorporated was no more. It wasn't the end of Damian Wayne though. When his corpse was taken to Darkseid's home of Apokolips, Batman followed and, after a ferocious struggle, not only retrieved it but also gained the power to resurrect either his parents or Damian. He chose Damian and brought his son back to life.

THE LAST LAUGH

The Joker survived his fall in the Batcave and unleashed a new Joker virus on Gotham City, driving the population into insane, laughing killers. As Batman and his allies struggled to find a cure, the Dark Knight was forced to call on both allies and enemies to help him. Batman eventually managed to locate a cure, deep in the caverns under Gotham, but was trapped there following explosions after one of his most brutal fights with the Joker. His allies took over his crime-fighting duties for a while but it wasn't long before Bruce Wayne returned to the cowl and Batman once again watched over Gotham City.

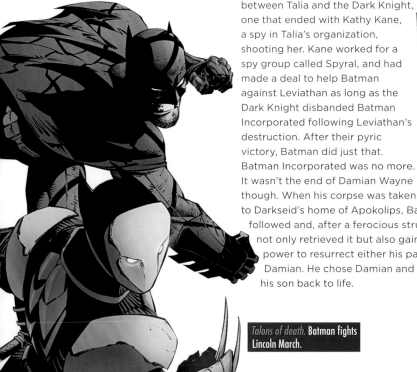

Talons of death. Batman fights Lincoln March.

To the end. Batman and the Joker slug it out in the caverns of Gotham.

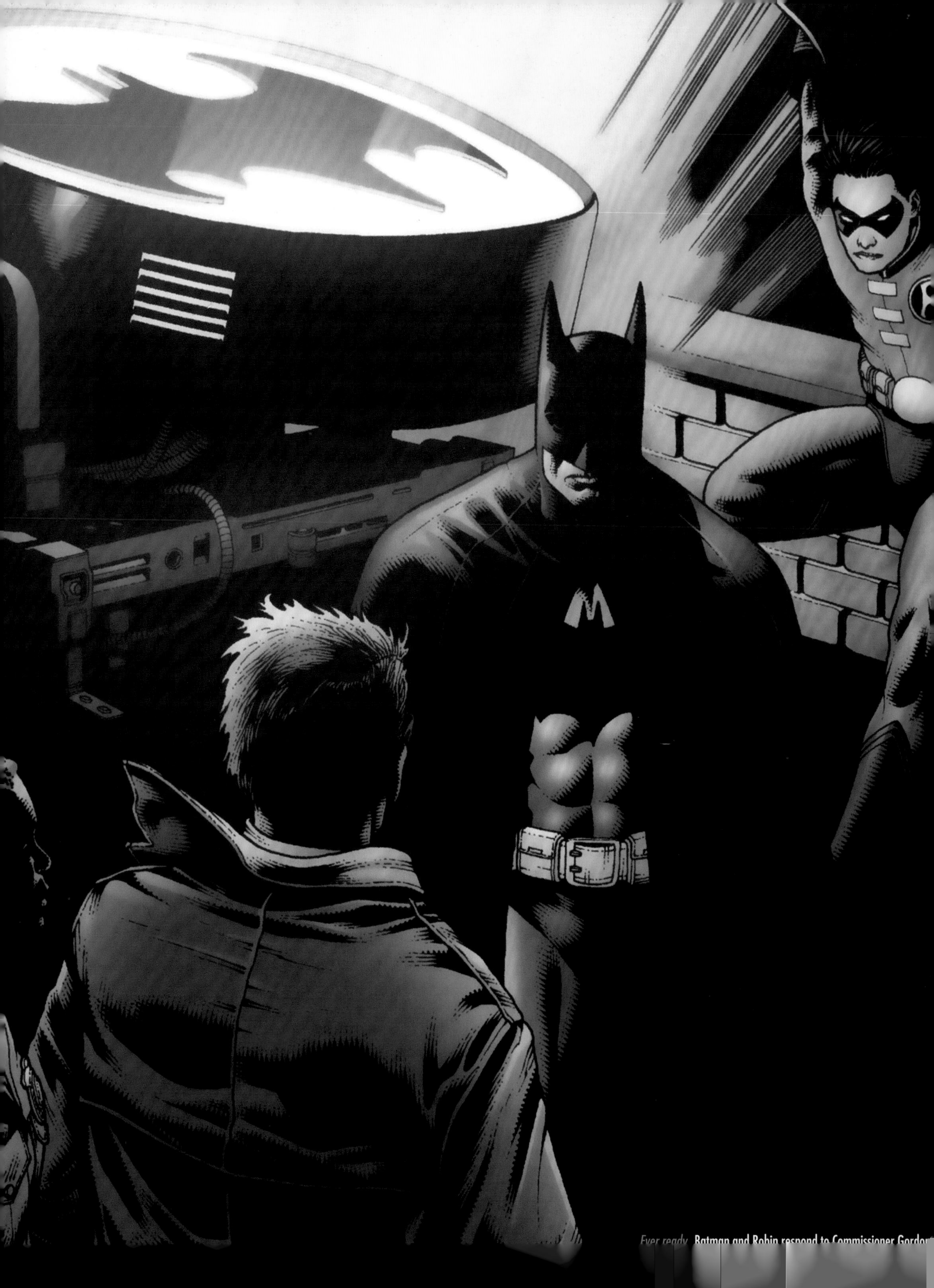

Ever ready Batman and Robin respond to Commissioner Gordon

LIGHT OF HOPE

FEW OBJECTS USED TO AID THE DARK KNIGHT'S FIGHT AGAINST CRIME HAVE BECOME AS ICONIC AS THE BAT-SIGNAL. FROM ITS HUMBLE BEGINNINGS AS A WAY OF CALLING TO BATMAN, IT HAS BECOME PART OF THE GOTHAM CITY SKYLINE...

To some it is an unwelcome spotlight on their dubious activities. To others it is a cherished beacon of hope. To one man in particular it is an urgent call to arms.

The Bat-Signal is a modified Klieg searchlight, most often affixed to the rooftop of the Gotham City Police Department Headquarters. A powerful carbon-arc lamp, it projects a large bat symbol onto the side of buildings or into the sky above Gotham City. Police Commissioner James Gordon uses the Bat-Signal to summon Batman in the event of a crisis – but he also uses the spotlight as a weapon of psychological intimidation. As Bruce Wayne once reflected, "criminals are a superstitious cowardly lot," and the light of the Bat-Signal piercing the darkness is often enough to make would-be wrongdoers think twice. It is a vivid reminder that Gotham City has a nocturnal defender – a heroic Dark Knight who will stop at nothing to protect the innocent and bring felons to justice.

MODERN MYTH

In the early days of his crime-fighting career, Batman was considered by many to be little more than an urban legend – a modern myth concocted by nervous hoodlums. However, as Gotham City's old-style mobsters, such as Carmine Falcone, gave way to a new breed of costumed super-villains, confirmed sightings of the Dark Knight increased.

And for the first time in weeks, people in my city are looking up...

In this new world, with men like the Joker and whatever else may be headed our way, that's a small victory, I know.

Signal of fear. Bruce Wayne looks on as the Scarecrow issues his challenge to Batman555

When the malevolent Joker plotted to poison the water supply of Gotham, Batman was forced out of the shadows and into the full glare of the media spotlight. Despite the unaccustomed attention, Batman managed to foil the Joker's evil scheme, successfully delivering the villain into the hands of the Gotham City Police Department. Many hailed Batman as a true hero, and the mayor seized upon the opportunity for positive publicity by suggesting that the GCPD keep informal links with the Dark Knight. James Gordon – who had already been working with Batman in secret – was assigned as the Dark Knight's police liaison, charged with operating the newly created Bat-Signal.

The Bat-Signal soon became a reassuring feature of Gotham City life – at least to the vast majority of law-abiding citizens. To the crooked

Signing out. Batman discovers the Scarecrow's Halloween lantern.

minority, however, both the Bat-Signal and James Gordon became the targets of their ire. On one occasion, the demented Scarecrow kidnapped Gordon. He then transformed the Bat-Signal into an enormous Halloween symbol – projecting a leering jack-o'-lantern into the sky as an overt challenge to Batman.

THE CHALLENGE ACCEPTED

The Dark Knight picked up the gauntlet, freeing Gordon and dispatching the Scarecrow to Arkham Asylum. Sometime later, Batman was also held captive – trapped by the Signalman within the Bat-Signal itself. Should James Gordon arrive to activate the device, he would unwittingly kill his friend. Fortunately, Batman broke free in spectacular fashion. He shattered the Bat-Signal's glass frontage – going on to shatter the Signalman's villainous ambitions.

When a mysterious individual called Mr. Whisper targeted Gotham City's mob bosses for assassination, the terrified hoodlums turned to Batman for help. They constructed their own version of the Bat-Signal, projecting the image of an inverted bat into the night sky. Batman responded to the call, and although he eventually went on to defeat Mr. Whisper, he also made a solemn vow to the mobsters. Should they ever pervert the image of the Bat-Signal in such a way again, they would suffer his wrath as never before.

Crime aid. The city's mob bosses shine an inverted Bat-Signal over the skies of Gotham.

WHAT--?!?

'S BEEN *SHORT-CIRCUITED!* BUT WHAT IN BLAZES COULD HAVE *DONE...*

WOULD YOU BELIEVE A PIECE OF *HEAVY-DUTY WIRE,* COMMISSIONER?

SKRASHHH!

BATMAN?!? BUT HOW--?!?

reakout. Batman foils the Signalman's plans by escaping his trap.

A SIGNAL TO NOISE

The Bat-Signal was damaged when a cataclysmic earthquake laid waste to Gotham City. The relationship between James Gordon and Batman was also broken. Bruce Wayne believed that he could best serve the interests of Gotham City by travelling to Washington in order to petition the US government for aid. However, when Gordon made repeated attempts to contact the Dark Knight he received no answer – and he came to believe that Batman had abandoned the city. When a junior police officer constructed a makeshift Bat-Signal, Gordon's anger boiled over – and he smashed the improvised device to pieces.

In the end, Bruce Wayne's efforts to secure help for Gotham City proved futile. The federal authorities abandoned the city to its fate – declaring it a lawless No Man's Land. Wayne refused to give in, however, and he returned home to his beloved city. As Batman, he set about re-establishing the rule of law – and was eventually reconciled with James Gordon, who had also been working tirelessly to turn back the tide of chaos. Following the restoration of civil society in Gotham, the authorities added a new Bat-Signal to the roof of the renovated Police HQ.

ILLUMINATING EVENTS

The Bat-Signal went unheeded when Bruce Wayne found himself incarcerated in Blackgate Penitentiary. Framed for the murder of broadcaster Vesper Fairchild by assassin David Cain, Wayne was locked up pending

Return of the hero. **After time away, Batman reappears over Gotham City.**

trial. From behind the bars of his cell he coul[d] see the Bat-Signal illuminating the night sky – urging the Dark Knight to attend Police H[Q] – but there was nothing he could do about i[t] Eventually, though, Wayne escaped from prison. He gathered enough evidence to pr[ove] his innocence, and Batman was once again free to answer the siren call of the Bat-Signa[l].

For a time, Michael Akins replaced James Gordon as Gotham City Police Commission[er] Akins cut all ties with the Dark Knight, demonstrating his disapproval of costumed vigilantes by dismantling the Bat-Signal. Shortly after this, Batman suffered a crisis o[f] faith. The super-human world had been rock[ed] by a number of tragic events, and Batman h[ad] lost his edge. He embarked on a journey to t[he] far corners of the world, hoping the trip wou[ld] rekindle his fighting spirit. By the time a reinvigorated Dark Knight returned to his cit[y] the Bat-Signal had not been seen in the skie[s] of Gotham City for many months.

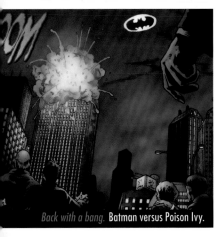

Back with a bang. Batman versus Poison Ivy.

began with a new beacon lighting up the heavens – an owl-signal. Fortunately, Batman was able to rally his allies, such as Nightwing, Batgirl and Robin, and save some – if not all – of the intended victims. The first clash between Batman and the Court of Owls was ultimately inconclusive – and just which is the most potent symbol, bat or owl, has yet to be fully determined.

With the creation of Batman Inc. – the international organization founded by Bruce Wayne and intended to take the Dark Knight's war on crime to the next level – the Bat-Signal took on new meaning. It became a globally recognized symbol of hope, a sign that evildoers could no longer operate with impunity. Whenever – and wherever – the Bat-Signal lights up the darkness, justice is now guaranteed to follow.

...mes Gordon was once again Police ...ommissioner, however, and when the ...o-terrorist Poison Ivy attacked a business ...elegation, he reactivated the Bat-Signal. The ...assuring sight of the bat-symbol beaming ...rough the darkness prompted cheers from ...any of Gotham City's citizens.

...MBOLS

...tman's world was rocked to its foundations ...hen he discovered that the legendary Court ...Owls was actually real – and that the ...andestine organization had been ...anipulating events within Gotham City for ...nturies. A secret cabal of the rich and ...werful, the Court of Owls was determined ...prove itself the true face of Gotham City, ...d to this end it captured and tortured ...tman. During the eight days of the Dark ...ight's torment, James Gordon ran the ...t-Signal continuously. In the end, the ...achine burned itself out – and there was still ...answer from the Dark Knight.

...Batman's eventual escape prompted the ...urt of Owls to unleash its Talons – an ...my of undying assassins with orders to ...minate Gotham's most civic-minded ...izens. The so-called Night of the Owls

CRIME BEWARE!

WHEREVER YOU ARE, BATMAN IS WATCHING!

LORD DEATH MAN'S A GUEST OF THE JAPANESE *SPACE PROGRAM* NOW.

SO I SUPPOSE THAT LEAVES JUST *ONE* LOOSE END, SELINA.

IT DOES, DOES IT?

LOOK, I'LL MISS MY FLIGHT...

Batman Inc. The Bat-Signal goes international.

Owl meets Bat. Batman comes up against the Court of Owls' assassins.

...ight of the Owls. Batgirl comes to the aid of ...atman as the owl-signal shines.

1. Commissioner Gordon lights the Bat-Signal nightly in support of Batman.

2. The Bat-Signal burns out.

3. Jean Paul Valley as Batman.

4. The Riddler's Bat-Signal.

5. Gordon and Nightwing discover the Black Mask's handiwork.

ANSWERING THE CALL

THE BAT–SIGNAL LIGHTING UP THE NIGHT SKY IS OFTEN THE CUE FOR THE DARK KNIGHT TO SWING INTO ACTION. HOWEVER, THERE HAVE BEEN MANY OTHERS WHO HAVE ALSO RESPONDED TO THE SPOTLIGHT'S SIREN CALL.

1. BECOMING THE KNIGHT

Dick Grayson was the original Robin, the Boy Wonder – and as such, he was the first person, other than Batman, to answer the call of the Bat-Signal. Police Commissioner James Gordon was initially appalled that the Dark Knight had taken on such a young crime-fighting partner. However, when he realized that Batman and Robin were father and son in all but name, he soon changed his mind. Years later, Dick temporarily took over the role of the Dark Knight. Gordon activated the Bat-Signal on a nightly basis to show his support for the 'new' Batman.

2. THE MASK SLIPS

While operating as Batman, Dick chose Bruce Wayne's biological son, Damian, as his new Robin. Damian was wilful and headstrong, prone to violent outbursts – and Dick sought to teach the youngster how to be a true hero. When Bruce Wayne donned the Dark Knight's cape and cowl once more, Damian remained as Robin. He often responded to the Bat-Signal alongside his father – and joined Commissioner Gordon in a rooftop vigil at Police HQ when Batman mysteriously disappeared. Gordon had been running the Bat-Signal continuously for eight days. When the machine finally gave up the ghost, Damian demanded that it be replaced immediately – and that the police continue in their efforts to contact the Dark Knight. In that moment, Damian's arrogant mask slipped... and his true feelings were revealed for perhaps the first time.

3. IN THE SPOTLIGHT

Jean Paul Valley took over the role of Gotham's nocturnal guardian when Bruce Wayne's body and spirit were broken by the villainous Bane. With "The System" – an arcane mix of physical and psychological training – driving him on, Valley became an even darker Dark Knight. He redesigned the Batsuit, transforming it into a fearsome-looking piece of battle armour. Gordon continued to use the Bat-Signal to contact Batman – but he soon realized that his old friend was no longer wearing the cape and cowl. When Valley's crime-fighting methods became too extreme, Gordon vowed to bring the out-of-control vigilante to justice.

4. QUESTIONS

On the trail of a murderer dubbed the 'Hangman', Batman made the surprising move of asking the Riddler for help. Although the self-styled Prince of Puzzles was unable to deduce Hangman's secret identity, he did provide information that ultimately led to the villain's defeat. The Riddler used the Bat-Signal to contact the Dark Knight. He modified the machine to project the image of a question mark into the night sky – much to Batman's ire, who shattered the new lens with a well-placed Batarang. Sometime later, Charles Victor Sage also used the Bat-Signal to project a question mark into the heavens above Gotham City. His message was intended for former GCPD officer Renee Montoya – challenging her to become his replacement as the masked hero known only as the Question.

5. GOTHAM NETWORK

When Batman was mistakenly believed dead at the hands of the New God called Darkseid, criminals ran amok in Gotham City. The villainous Black Mask orchestrated a mass breakout at Arkham Asylum, and altered the Bat-Signal so that it projected the letters RIP into the night sky. At the sight of this, the city's criminal element became even more emboldened – and the Police Department struggled to stem the rising tide of chaos. However, villains weren't the only ones to respond to the new signal, and Dick Grayson rallied Batman's protégés and allies in the defence of Gotham City. In the guise of Nightwing, he successfully melded the likes of Batwoman, Robin, Tim Drake and Catwoman into an effective fighting force, dubbing his compatriots the Gotham Network. After helping to restore order, Nightwing realized that it was his destiny to take up the mantle of Batman.

1. Home of the Miagani Tribe.

2. Garage and hangar.

3. Global monitoring station.

4. Modern eight-level design.

THE BATCAVE

THE BATCAVE IS A GARAGE FOR ALL OF BATMAN'S TRANSPORT, FROM BATMOBILES TO BATCOPTERS. IT ALSO ACTS AS A TRAINING FACILITY, AND AS A MEDICAL CENTER WITH ALFRED ON HAND TO PERFORM FIRST AID.

1. ANCIENT ORIGINS

Batman's recent travels in time have shed new light on the cave's history. An amnesiac Bruce Wayne first lived in the caves after arriving in prehistoric Gotham City, leaving ancient drawings of the bat insignia on the wall. His appearance and costume gave rise to a bat-cult whose members lived in the caves. In the 17th century, the caves were home to the Miagani tribe – also known as the Bat-people. Batman met the tribe while trying to lead Blackbeard to treasure hidden in the cave. The treasure turned out to be Batman's cowl, left there by himself in prehistory. Centuries later, during the Civil War, the cave system was used by the Wayne family as part of the Underground Railroad to help escaped slaves.

2. HI-TECH HANGAR

Early in his career, Bruce used the caves as a sanctum, but he soon realized their potential as a base of operations. Over the years the Batcave has been expanded from a makeshift storage facility into a hi-tech strategic centre, whence Batman can monitor events across the world. When the base was destroyed by an earthquake that devastated Gotham City, Batman used it as an opportunity to rebuild and update the Batcave's operating systems and make the most of its vast space. (Should such disaster strike again, Batman has several secret satellite caves scattered around the globe. One is located directly beneath Arkham Asylum, another under the Robinson Park Reservoir in Gotham.)

The modern-day Batcave is constructed over eight levels and stretches almost a mile beneath Wayne Manor. A series of retractable walkways, lifts, stairs and poles link the different levels, while the cave's energy supply comes from multiple hydrogen generators. There are also sleeping quarters and refreshment areas, and several entrances and exits, each guarded by highly advanced security measures. (In Wayne Manor, one secret entrance is behind a grandfather clock, its face is set at 10:47, the time Thomas and Martha Wayne were killed.) There is a specially designed hangar for Batman's many vehicles and a hi-tech research center for upgrading them. Each of these vehicles – from Batmobiles through to the Batwing (Batman's supersonic jet) – has its own concealed exit point from the cave. (Batman's vehicles were once maintained by Harold Allnut, a mute and hunchbacked technological genius. However, Harold betrayed Batman's secrets to Hush, who then killed him.)

The Batcave's new design makes full use of the cave's height and includes areas given over to fitness training, forensics, medical facilities, and a vast library. The Batcave also has a Justice League teleporter, allowing Batman instant access to the JLA. (On that note, the cave also houses a containment centre that keeps various forms of Kryptonite in safe storage, a very practical help to Superman.)

3. CENTRAL COMPUTER

The heart of the Batcave is Batman's highly advanced computer system, constructed on an island platform. The system is powered by seven Cray T392 mainframes and includes a holographic projector. Containing a vast archive on Batman's enemies and allies, plus a huge record of crimes and cases, it is one of the most powerful computers in the world. (Possibly only the JLA's computer, which utilizes alien technology, is more advanced.) The computer platform is protected from earthquake and attack by Kevlar shielding.

4. TROPHIES & TROGLODYTES

Batman keeps several trophies from early adventures in the Batcave. These include a life-sized robotic T-Rex, a giant penny and oversized playing card from the Joker. Barbara Gordon's Batgirl costume is on display alongside Jason Todd's Robin outfit (despite the latter's return from the grave). There is also a collection of ancient armor.

Last but not least, the cave is still home to a colony of bats. They seem to have grown used to sharing their home with the hero whose identity they inspired.

Dinosaur Island Souvenir.

THE WEAPONS MASTER. THE KEY. NOW SCARECROW, THE SCAVENGER, CAPTAIN COLD, THE CHEETAH...

...THERE'VE BEEN OVER A DOZEN REPORTS OF OUR ENEMIES BEING ATTACKED, TORTURED AND INTERROGATED BY SOMEONE NAMED *GRAVES.*

1. Batman briefs the Justice League.

STOP, SUPERMAN. *PLEASE.*

WE'RE NOT WORKING WITH THOSE FIRE-BREATHING *MONSTERS.* WE WERE ATTACKED. *JUST LIKE YOU.*

GREEN LANTERN'S RING SAID THEY WERE *ALIEN.* WE THOUGHT MAYBE YOU WOULD KNOW WHAT THEY WERE.

UH, *YEAH.* WHAT BATMAN SAID.

2. A situation is defused between Superman and Green Lantern.

3. Batman's stash of emergency weapons.

4. Superman helps Batman quell the Arkham Asylum riots.

5. Aquaman and B don't always see ey

A LEAGUE AHEAD

BATMAN IS THE CALM AT THE CENTER OF A RAGING STORM. HIS TACTICAL ACUMEN AND FORWARD THINKING HAVE MADE HIM THE STANDOUT LEADER OF THE JUSTICE LEAGUE.

1. MASTER PLANNER

The Dark Knight is a superior tactician and a master strategist. He knows that any campaign is won or lost in the planning stages – and he uses his amazing investigative skills to ensure that the Justice League is fully prepared before entering the field. Only when all the available facts have been logged and reviewed will Batman risk leading the team into action. During Darkseid's attempted invasion of Earth, Batman forged the disparate heroes into an effective fighting force – and in the five years since, his analytical mind has proven invaluable to the team.

2. VOICE OF REASON

The Justice League is a team of super heroes – though some would characterize it as a team of giant egos! From the very beginning, the group has risked falling into fractious in-fighting. Without doubt the most argumentative members are Green Lantern and Aquaman – both of whom believe they should be the one to lead the team. In this highly charged atmosphere, Batman has proven to be a voice of reason. When the heroes first met, he broke up a physical confrontation between Superman and Green Lantern – and ensured that the team kept focused while battling the forces of Darkseid. Accustomed to operating in the shadows, the Dark Knight realizes that it is not the individual who is important, but the successful conclusion of the mission.

3. TRUST NO ONE

Batman plans for every eventuality – and while he respects his Justice League teammates, he has formulated weapons and contingencies to take down his fellow heroes should they ever turn rogue and threaten humanity. The weapons were kept in a supposedly top-secret vault in the Batcave, but a mysterious infiltrator broke in to steal a ring fashioned from Kryptonite that could prove deadly to Superman. Batman's distrust even extends to the United Nations and its operatives. When the Justice League International group was founded under the auspices of the UN, Batman forced his way onto the team to monitor its activities.

4. LUNCH BUDDIES

Batman and Superman share a unique bond, often teaming up to operate beyond the confines of the Justice League. And while the Dark Knight might deny that the Man of Steel is his friend, Superman certainly thinks of Batman as more than a mere comrade-in-arms. He turned to Batman when seeking advice on his secret identity, and he considers the Dark Knight one of the smartest men in the world. In turn, Batman often calls in Superman to help solve particularly troublesome cases. They quelled a riot in Arkham Asylum while on a lunch break, and teamed up to investigate a spate of mysterious disappearances in Gotham City.

5. BURDEN OF LEADERSHIP

Aquaman was always a vocal critic of the Dark Knight's leadership techniques and command decisions. However, in the wake of an aborted attempt by the city of Atlantis to invade the surface world, Aquaman now finds himself the sole ruler of the vast undersea kingdom. He now appreciates the difficult choices the Dark Knight has had to make, and he finally understands that leadership can sometimes be a lonely burden.

2. Stately Wayne Manor.

THAT *WILL* BE ALL, MASTER BRUCE? I'M HOPING THAT THE NEXT GENERATION OF THE WAYNE FAMILY SHANT FACE AN EMPTY WINE CELLAR.

THOUGH GIVEN YOUR SOCIAL SCHEDULE OF LATE, THE PROSPECTS OF THERE *BEING* A NEXT GENERATION--

THAT WILL BE ALL, ALFRED. GOOD NIGHT.

WARNING

DESTRUCT SEQUENCE

AFFIRMAT

DANGER

TK TK TK

Alfred sets the self-destruct for Wayne Manor.

1. Rioting on the West Side.

3. Bruce Wayne Crime Alley.

THE *DUMP* STRETCHES OUT OF SIGHT FROM THE FAR BANK OF THE *WEST RIVER.* I'M TOLD IT ENDS SOMEWHERE BEFORE THE *FARMLANDS.*

IT SMELLS OF *ROT* AND *RUST--* IT'S A *BREEDING GROUND* FOR *INSECTS* AND *RODENTS.*

I CUT THE *ENGINE* AND LISTEN TO ONE OF THE *RODENTS.*

THEY CALL US A GANG. THEY CALL US A MOB. THEY THINK WE JUST NOISY KIDS.

ONLY WHEN THEY *DIE* BY OUR *HANDS* AND SEE THEIR WOMEN *RAPED* WILL THEY KNOW...

--WE HAVE THE *STRENGTH--* WE HAVE THE *WILL--* AND NOW WE HAVE THE *GUNS.*

GOTHAM CITY BELONGS TO

FREE COTTON CANDY FREE

4. The Dump — Mutant home.

5. The Joker hands out deadly candy at Gotham County Fair.

CITY IN DECLINE

THE GOTHAM CITY OF THE DARK KNIGHT RETURNS IS A
CITY IN SEEMINGLY TERMINAL DECAY, WITH MANY AREAS
BECOMING MORE DANGEROUS THAN EVER BEFORE.

1. THE WEST SIDE
Home to former Police Commissioner
James Gordon and his wife, Sarah, the
West Side was a relatively prosperous
area – but even it was not immune to the
chaotic lawlessness that was endemic to
Gotham City. During a blackout caused
by the detonation of a nuclear missile,
rioting broke out in the West Side – with
terrified mobs fighting over food and
other valuable resources. Appalled at
the behavior of his fellow Gothamites,
James Gordon convinced the rioters to
listen to the better part of their natures –
organizing them into a task force to put
out the fires and to provide first aid to
the wounded.

2. WAYNE MANOR
Home to many generations of the family
from which it took its name, Wayne
Manor overlooked Gotham City from
Crest Hill for over 150 years. When
Bruce Wayne first donned the cape
and cowl of the Dark Knight, Wayne
Manor became a secret home to
Batman. Excavating the limestone
caverns beneath the building and the
surrounding estate, Bruce created a
Batcave for his alter ego. It became
a high-tech base of operations from
where he could wage his war on
crime, often with the assistance of
Alfred Pennyworth – the Wayne
family's ever-loyal butler. After
faking Batman's death, Bruce
realized that his true identity would
be exposed, and so he ordered
Alfred to blow up Wayne Manor in
order to prevent its subterranean
secrets from falling into the wrong
hands. Rather poignantly, the
aged Alfred died peacefully as
the flames consumed his home of
many decades.

3. CRIME ALLEY
Crime Alley was formerly the prestigious
Park Row, but its glamorous façade was
tarnished forever when Bruce Wayne's
parents were murdered on its neon-lit
cobbles. Over the years, the surrounding
area became synonymous with lawlessness
– and by the time of *The Dark Knight
Returns*, only a madman would take a
late-night stroll through Crime Alley. Ten
years after his retirement as Batman, that
decision weighing heavily on his conscience,
Bruce Wayne absent-mindedly returned to
Crime Alley – where he came face-to-face
with a group of outlaw Mutants. That
potentially lethal encounter sparked a
sequence of events that eventually led to
the Dark Knight's rebirth. Some time later,
Batman chose Crime Alley as a fitting
location for his final confrontation with
Superman.

4. WEST RIVER DUMP
There was never a more appropriate location
for the human vermin of the Mutant
gang to congregate than the West River
Dump – a notorious breeding ground
for disease-ridden rodents. The Mutant
Leader issued a challenge for Batman
to meet his savage gang at the dump –
which the Dark Knight gladly accepted,
driving into combat behind the wheel of
an enormous tank-like Batmobile. Batman
used the vehicle's heavy-caliber weapons to
cut through the ranks of the Mutants, and to
effectively destroy them as a fighting force.
Some time later, the dump became a staging
post for the Dark Knight's campaign to
restore law and order to a chaotic
Gotham City.

5. GOTHAM COUNTY FAIR
One of the few bright spots of Gotham City,
the celebrated County Fair descended into
chaos when the Joker embarked on a
murderous rampage. After spending ten
years as a docile patient in Arkham Asylum,
the Joker awoke from a near-catatonic
stupor upon hearing the news of the Dark
Knight's return. He attempted to blow up
many hundreds of innocent people at the
County Fair, but with Batman hot on his
heels he sought sanctuary in the darkened
caverns of the Tunnel of Love. After years of
enmity, the final confrontation between
Batman and the Joker ended with the death
of the Clown Prince of Crime – and the Dark
Knight hunted by the authorities.

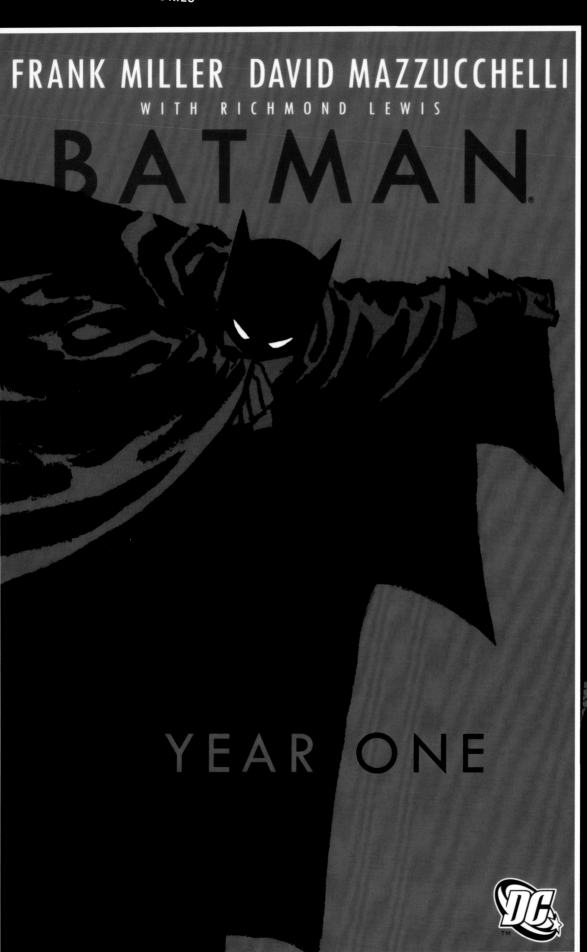

FRANK MILLER   DAVID MAZZUCCHELLI

WITH RICHMOND LEWIS

BATMAN

YEAR ONE

Batman:
Year One was adapted into a DC Universe animated movie in 2011, with stars Bryan Cranston and Eliza Dushku providing voices.

BATMAN: YEAR ONE

(*BATMAN* #404-407) FEBRUARY-MAY 1987

BATMAN: YEAR ONE was written by Frank Miller and illustrated by David Mazzucchelli. The story dealt with Bruce Wayne's first outings as the Dark Knight and Jim Gordon's first months with the Gotham City Police Department. The city was filled with corruption, from the police dept to the Falcone crime family, with Wayne and Gordon two of the few men to make a stand against it. The young Bruce Wayne soon learned he needed an edge to help his fight and, inspired by a bat crashing through a window in Wayne Manor, became Batman. At the same time Jim Gordon realized just how corrupt GCPD was. Their paths met in a powerful climax that signalled the start of their alliance.

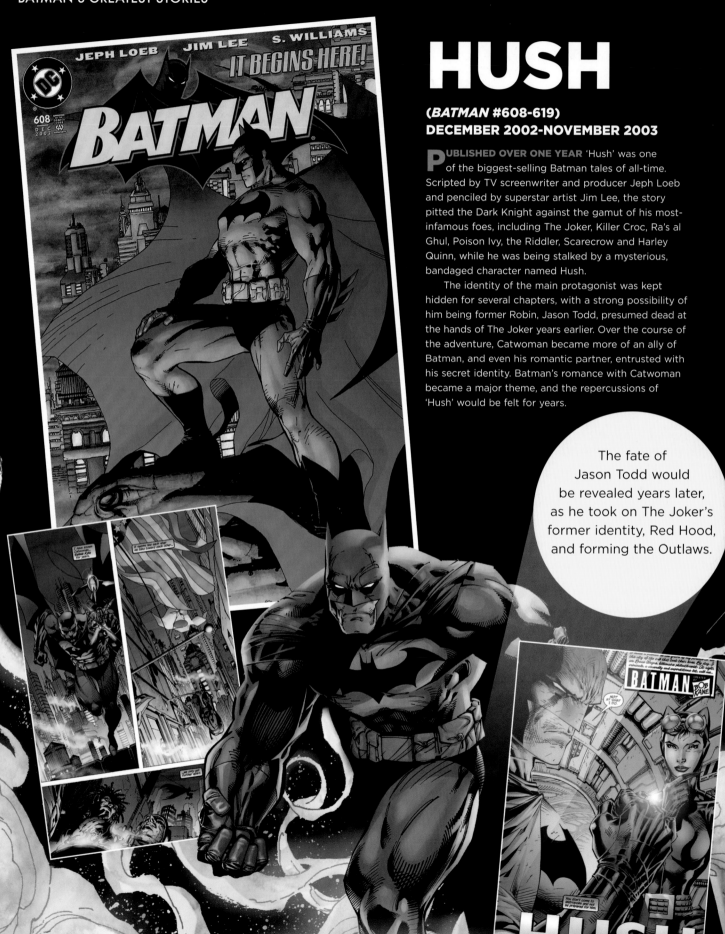

HUSH

(*BATMAN* #608-619)
DECEMBER 2002-NOVEMBER 2003

PUBLISHED OVER ONE YEAR 'Hush' was one of the biggest-selling Batman tales of all-time. Scripted by TV screenwriter and producer Jeph Loeb and penciled by superstar artist Jim Lee, the story pitted the Dark Knight against the gamut of his most-infamous foes, including The Joker, Killer Croc, Ra's al Ghul, Poison Ivy, the Riddler, Scarecrow and Harley Quinn, while he was being stalked by a mysterious, bandaged character named Hush.

The identity of the main protagonist was kept hidden for several chapters, with a strong possibility of him being former Robin, Jason Todd, presumed dead at the hands of The Joker years earlier. Over the course of the adventure, Catwoman became more of an ally of Batman, and even his romantic partner, entrusted with his secret identity. Batman's romance with Catwoman became a major theme, and the repercussions of 'Hush' would be felt for years.

The fate of Jason Todd would be revealed years later, as he took on The Joker's former identity, Red Hood, and forming the Outlaws.

THE COURT OF OWLS

(*BATMAN* VOL.2 #1-7)
NOVEMBER 2011-MAY 2012

THE DC COMICS: the New 52 timeline reboot in 2011 introduced an exciting new partnership between writer Scott Snyder and artist Greg Capullo. The Court of Owls saga revealed a secret society which had been manipulating Gotham City for decades. Bruce Wayne's own ancestors knew of them and Dick (Nightwing) Grayson's family were also connected, but it took some time for the Dark Knight to become convinced of their existence. Attacked by the Court's immortal enforcer, the Talon, then taken prisoner, the Dark Knight underwent a tough psychological battle to stay alive and escape from the Court of Owls' deadly labyrinth.

DC COMICS

THE NEW 52

BATMAN

VOLUME
THE COURT OF OWL

"SNYDER MIGHT BE THE DEFINING BATMAN WRITER OF OUR GENERATION."
— COMPLEX MAGAZINE

ENOUGH!

WELCOME, BATMAN, TO THE LABYRINTH!

SNYDER   GREG CAPULLO   JONATHAN GLAPION

The tale adds a new dimension to Batman's origin, with the young Bruce Wayne suspecting the Owls of orchestrating his parents' murder.

BATMAN

WITH SUPERB DETECTIVE SKILLS AND DETERMINATION BATMAN DELIVERS JUSTICE TO A CRIME-RIDDEN CITY.

THE DARK KNIGHT'S early adventures saw him tackle Gotham City's gangster fraternity but before long he had a costumed cavalcade of villains to match his wits against, including the Joker, the Penguin, Catwoman and the Riddler. Taking on a young ward, Robin the Boy Wonder, Batman's adventures became lighter in tone, with alien encounters and forays into outer space. The Sixties saw him as a team-player regularly fighting alongside Superman, a young Batgirl and the Justice League of America.

The Seventies returned a solo Dark Knight, dealing with darker crimes, the manipulative Ra's al Ghul and tragic Man-Bat. Post-Crisis on Infinite Earths, Batman faced many dark days with the death of the second Robin, Jason Todd, and his own incapacitation at the hands of Bane. Gotham City, too, faced tragedies, including a plague and earthquake.

Throughout the darkness, the Bat-Signal has shone brightly, offering hope that the Dark Knight is battling to keep his city safe.

JIM LEE 2001

1941

1965

1970

1972

1988

1993

1996

2002

2011

GOLDEN AGE

FROM HIS DEBUT IN MAY 1939, BATMAN STRUCK A CHORD WITH COMIC-BOOK READERS.

LESS THAN A YEAR after the debut of Superman in *Action Comics* #1, a startlingly different superstar debuted in *Detective Comics* #27. In somber black and gray, this cowled hero was a creature of the night – the Bat-Man. Secretly the socialite businessman Bruce Wayne, he was a "mysterious and adventurous figure fighting for righteousness". Using his wits and fists alone, the Bat-Man was a grim detective who thwarted a sinister company takeover and murder, and regarded the ultimate death of the villain as a fitting end.

Batman finally received his origin tale in November 1939's *Detective Comics* #33. Recalling the gunning down of his wealthy parents 15 years earlier, Bruce Wayne swore an oath to avenge their deaths with a war on crime. Inspired by a bat flying through his mansion window, the young man chose a disguise to strike terror into the hearts of cowardly criminals.

Batman's character softened somewhat in *Detective Comics* #38 (April 1940) with the introduction of his sidekick, Robin the Boy Wonder. In *Batman* #1, the Dark Knight gained two foes, the Joker and the Cat (later Catwoman). In his Batcave base, Batman built up an armory of gadgets, a Batgyro and Batmobile, while his Rogue's Gallery was joined by Clayface (1940), Scarecrow and the Penguin (1941), Two-Face (1942), the Riddler and the Mad Hatter. (1948).

THE JOKER
arrives in *Batman* #1 (Spring 1940)

GOTHAM CITY
First named in *Batman* #4 (December 1940)

BATMOBILE
ridden into *Detective Comics* #48 (February 1941)

BAT-SIGNAL
shines in *Detective Comics* #60 (February 1942)

ALFRED
arrives at Wayne Manor in *Batman* #16 (April 1943)

ACE
The Bat-Hound joins the Caped Crusaders in *Batman* #92 (June 1955)

100
Batman celebrates one hundred issues (June 1956)

BATWOMAN
Kathy Kane dons a mask in *Detective Comics* #233

SILVER AGE

WITH A HIT TV SHOW ON AIR, BATMAN'S COMIC BOOK ADVENTURES REACHED A NEW HIGH OF POPULARITY AND GRAPHIC STORYTELLING.

MR. FREEZE
Mr. Zero, later Mr. Freeze puts Batman on ice,
Batman #121 (February 1959)

BAT-MITE
the interdimensional imp invades the Batcave,
Detective Comics #267 (May 1959)

New-look Batman, *Detective Comics* #327 (May 1964)

POW!
Premiere of *Batman* TV series (January 1966)

POISON IVY
enters Batman's Rogue's Gallery,
Batman #181 (June 1966)

BATGIRL
Barbara Gordon joins the Batman family,
Detective Comics #359 (January 1967)

HAPPY BIRTHDAY
Batman celebrates his 30th anniversary,
Detective Comics #387 (May 1969)

HUDSON U
Dick Grayson swaps the Batcave for university,
Detective Comics #394 (December 1969)

BATMAN WAS ONE of the few super heroes to survive the post-WWII years with continuous publication. While DC heroes, such as The Flash and Green Lantern, were revived in the late 50s with new costumes and new alter egos, the Caped Crusader remained fairly unscathed, having stayed a hugely popular character since his debut twenty years earlier. But, in 1964, exactly 300 issues of *Detective Comics* after his first appearance, Batman final got a revamp, with a yellow ellipse added to his chest logo, and sci-fi fables dropped in favor of a return to his detective roots. Batman also began appearing regularly in *The Brave and the Bold* #59 in May 1965, teaming up with DC Comics' multifarious heroes.

A light-hearted, pop art-styled TV show, launched in 1966, brought the comic books a new generation of fans but by 1968, a grittier tone was called for. The Dark Knight gained a thoroughly modern look and haunting series of new foes. The exit of Robin also led to Bruce Wayne quitting the Batcave for a penthouse base above the Wayne Foundation.

BRONZE AGE

BATMAN TITLES OF THE 1970S INTRODUCED NEW HORROR-INFLUENCED ENEMIES WHILE FAMILIAR FOES RETURNED IN A DARKER GUISE.

BATMAN'S ADVENTURES TOOK on a darker modern hue in the 1970s, under the stewardship of creators such as writers Dennis O'Neil and Frank Robbins, with artists Neal Adams and Irv Novick. New sinister villains Man-Bat and the global eco-terrorist Ra's al Ghul debuted, while both the Joker and Two-Face reemerged as less comic, deadlier opponents.

Ra's al Ghul, the Demon's Head, was one of the few villains to deduce that Batman's secret identity was Bruce Wayne. He manipulated the Dark Knight, trying to persuade him to become his heir as head of his Brotherhood. While Batman rejected al Ghul's methods, he was torn by his feelings for the Demon's daughter, Talia.

A classic eight-issue run by Steve Englehart and Marshall Rogers continued the revival of the Dark Knight Detective, bringing back Professor Hugo Strange, one of Batman's oldest enemies, who had been absent for nearly 37 years. Away from the

Batcave, Bruce Wayne finally handed over the day-to-day running of his Wayne Foundation to a new executive named Lucius Fox and, after several solo years, the Dark Knight gained a new Robin in the form of Jason Todd, a circus acrobat like his predecessor Dick Grayson.

MAN-BAT
arrives in *Detective Comics* #400 (June 1970)

DEMON
Ra's Al Ghul makes his play in *Batman* #232 (June 1971)

THE END
the Last Dark Knight story in *Batman* #300 (June 1978)

FRANK MILLER
draws the Dark Knight for the first time in *DC Special Series* #21 (April 1980)

UNTOLD
Legend of the Batman miniseries (July 1980)

ARKHAM ASYLUM
opens its doors in *Batman* #326 (August 1980)

500
Detective Comics #526 celebrates Batman's 500th appearance (1983)

JASON TODD
wears the Robin costume in *Batman* #366 (December 1983)

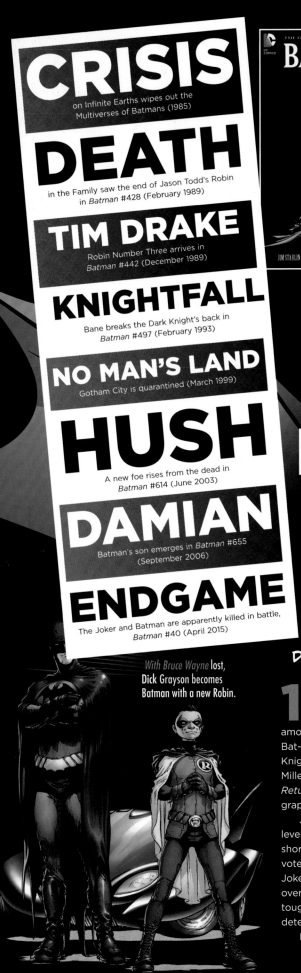

CRISIS
on Infinite Earths wipes out the Multiverses of Batmans (1985)

DEATH
in the Family saw the end of Jason Todd's Robin in *Batman* #428 (February 1989)

TIM DRAKE
Robin Number Three arrives in *Batman* #442 (December 1989)

KNIGHTFALL
Bane breaks the Dark Knight's back in *Batman* #497 (February 1993)

NO MAN'S LAND
Gotham City is quarantined (March 1999)

HUSH
A new foe rises from the dead in *Batman* #614 (June 2003)

DAMIAN
Batman's son emerges in *Batman* #655 (September 2006)

ENDGAME
The Joker and Batman are apparently killed in battle, *Batman* #40 (April 2015)

With *Bruce Wayne* lost, Dick Grayson becomes Batman with a new Robin.

MODERN AGE

THE CRISIS ON INFINITE EARTHS LED TO A SERIES OF CALAMITIES WHICH PUSHED THE DARK KNIGHT TO THE LIMITS.

1984-5'S CRISIS ON INFINITE EARTHS was a reboot for the DC Universe, wiping out the many Earths that contained, amongst others, the Golden-Age Batman, Bat-Mite and Ace the Bat-hound. The Dark Knight gained a grittier origin, care of Frank Miller, whose *Batman: The Dark Knight Returns* had won plaudits and invigorated the graphic-novel market.

Jason Todd's Robin had a new street-level origin, but his reign as Boy Wonder was short-lived as – thanks to a public phone vote – he died in an explosion set up by the Joker. It took a long time for Batman to get over the loss, with his adventures becoming tougher, his crackdown on crime even more determined than ever.

Finally a new Robin, Tim Drake, lightened the Dark Knight's mood but further calamities occurred: *Knightfall*, which saw Batman's back broken by Bane and a violent new Dark Knight arise; and *No Man's Land*, which left a ruined Gotham City isolated following a 7.5-magnitude earthquake.

Batman's apparent death at the hands of Darkseid led to Bruce Wayne struggling through history to reach the present, while Dick Grayson donned the cowl, with Bruce's son Damian, as a new Robin.

Following the events of Flashpoint, Batman was now the first super hero and haunted by a secret society called the Court of Owls. After a brief period with Commissioner James Gordon acting as Batman, Bruce Wayne returned as Gotham City's protector.

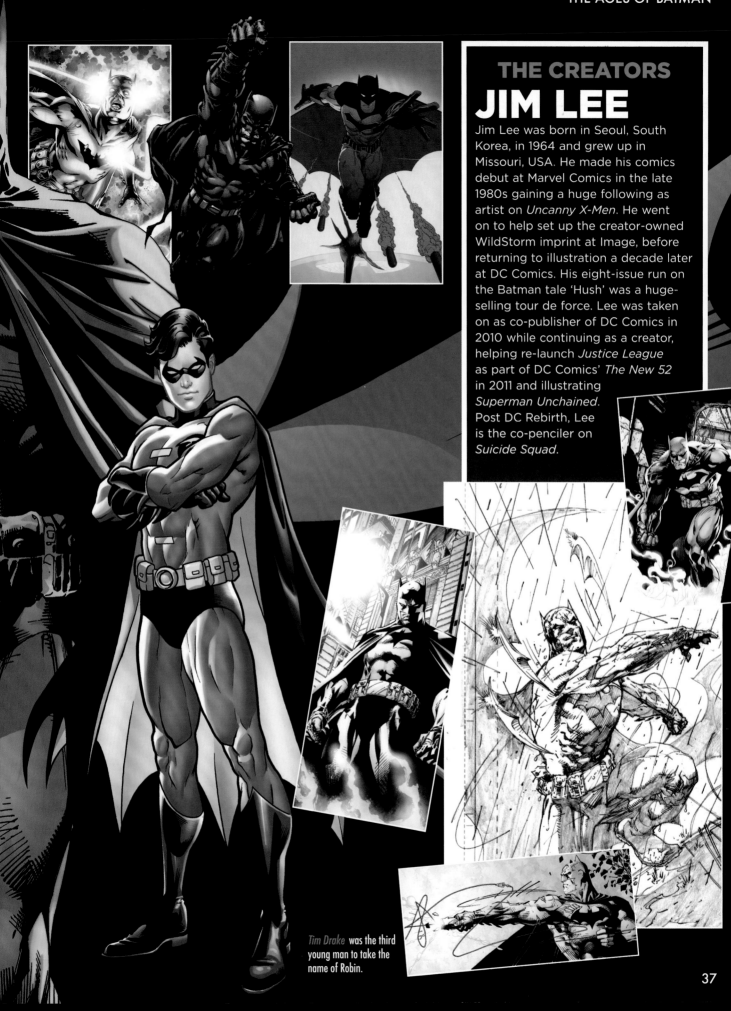

THE CREATORS
JIM LEE

Jim Lee was born in Seoul, South Korea, in 1964 and grew up in Missouri, USA. He made his comics debut at Marvel Comics in the late 1980s gaining a huge following as artist on *Uncanny X-Men*. He went on to help set up the creator-owned WildStorm imprint at Image, before returning to illustration a decade later at DC Comics. His eight-issue run on the Batman tale 'Hush' was a huge-selling tour de force. Lee was taken on as co-publisher of DC Comics in 2010 while continuing as a creator, helping re-launch *Justice League* as part of DC Comics' *The New 52* in 2011 and illustrating *Superman Unchained*. Post DC Rebirth, Lee is the co-penciler on *Suicide Squad*.

Tim Drake was the third young man to take the name of Robin.

THE JOKER

The Clown Prince of Cri[me]
is a deadly psychopath
responsible for countles[s]
deaths in Gotham City [and]
beyond. He is also Batm[an's]
deadliest enemy.
Presenting, The Joker...

MEET THE ACE OF KNAVES

THE JOKER: A DERANGED, SADISTIC KILLER WHO LIKES TO BRING HIS TWISTED SENSE OF HUMOR TO THE VICIOUS CRIMES HE COMMITS. WE TAKE A LOOK AT THE LIFE OF BATMAN'S GREATEST FOE...

There are some super-villains whose characters are scarred by unhappy childhoods or experiments that went wrong. There are others who are possessed by some character flaw that allows greed or revenge to overtake them; they give in to temptation or an obsessive nature and are consumed by them.

And then there is the Joker. If ever there has been a personification of a side of evil that is almost childlike in its straightforward, malignant glee, then it is Batman's oldest, deadliest enemy. Evil is often characterized as being banal and in the real world it often is: an accumulation of bad decisions, of good people looking the wrong way. Evil is inertia and, often, stupidity. But not in Batman's world. In the twilit domain of Gotham City, evil has both a dark glamor and a lurid appeal that is exemplified by the seething, labyrinthine mind and macabre style of the Clown Prince of Crime.

Batman's own personality has gradually changed over the decades, from a dedicated, brooding avenger to a darker, more earnest yet heroic personality. So too has the Joker's, except that his seems to be in permanent flux. As Batman's polar opposite, the Joker has evolved equal, utterly contrasting behaviors with which to deliver his own special brand of chaos. If Batman and his allies attempt to protect the innocent, the Joker attempts to subvert or slaughter them.

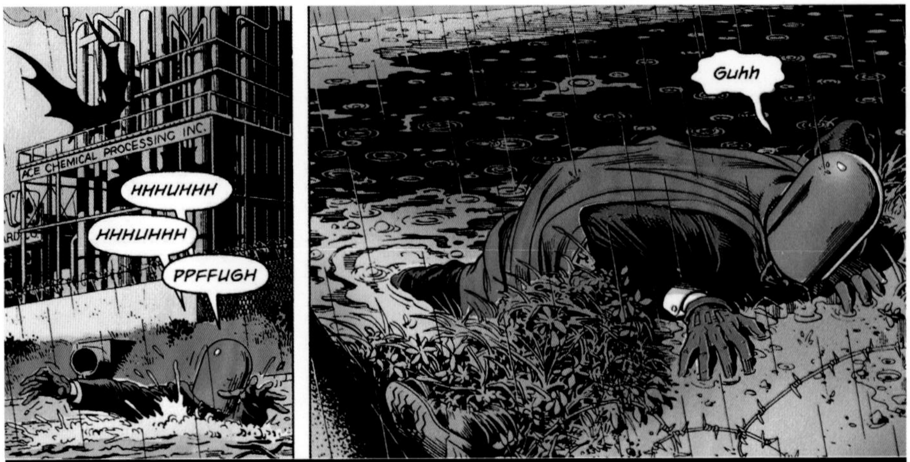
ACE CHEMICAL PROCESSING INC.
HHHUHHH
HHHUHHH
PPFFUGH
Guhh

The birth of the Joker. **According to some accounts, the Joker was once the Red Hood.**

ALL IT TAKES IS ONE BAD DAY ...

If the Joker's methodology grows evermore murderous, his pathological nature and his ultimate goal have always remained consistent: a desire to be Gotham's greatest criminal mastermind. Although details change, one origin of the Joker suggests that he once posed as a criminal known as the Red Hood. Or, to be precise, he was a failed stand-up comedian who had recently suffered the loss of his wife and unborn child. He was duped into taking on the persona of the Red Hood by a gang of thugs who needed a figurehead to divert attention away from themselves while robbing the Ace Chemical Plant. A former engineer at the plant, the "Red Hood" was confronted by Batman during the robbery and accidentally plummeted into a vat of chemicals. He emerged with his skin bleached white, his hair emerald green, and his mouth stretched permanently into a malevolent, red-lipped grin. In that instant he became the Joker, blaming Batman for his fall into the chemical mixture that changed him, and fixating upon the Dark Knight as his arch-enemy. Much of this scenario was later corroborated by Edward Nigma, aka the Riddler, who apparently observed the whole thing.

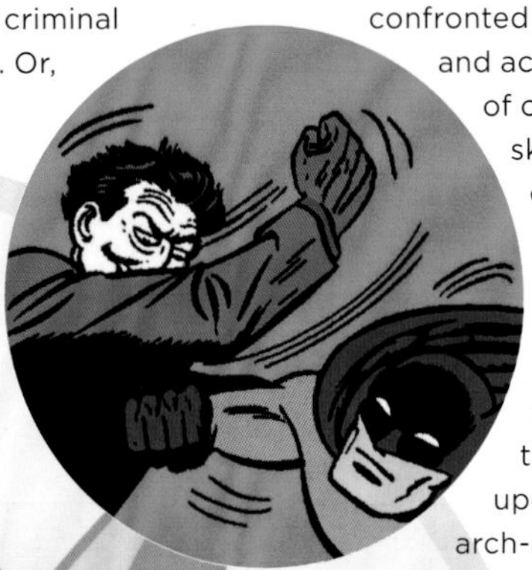

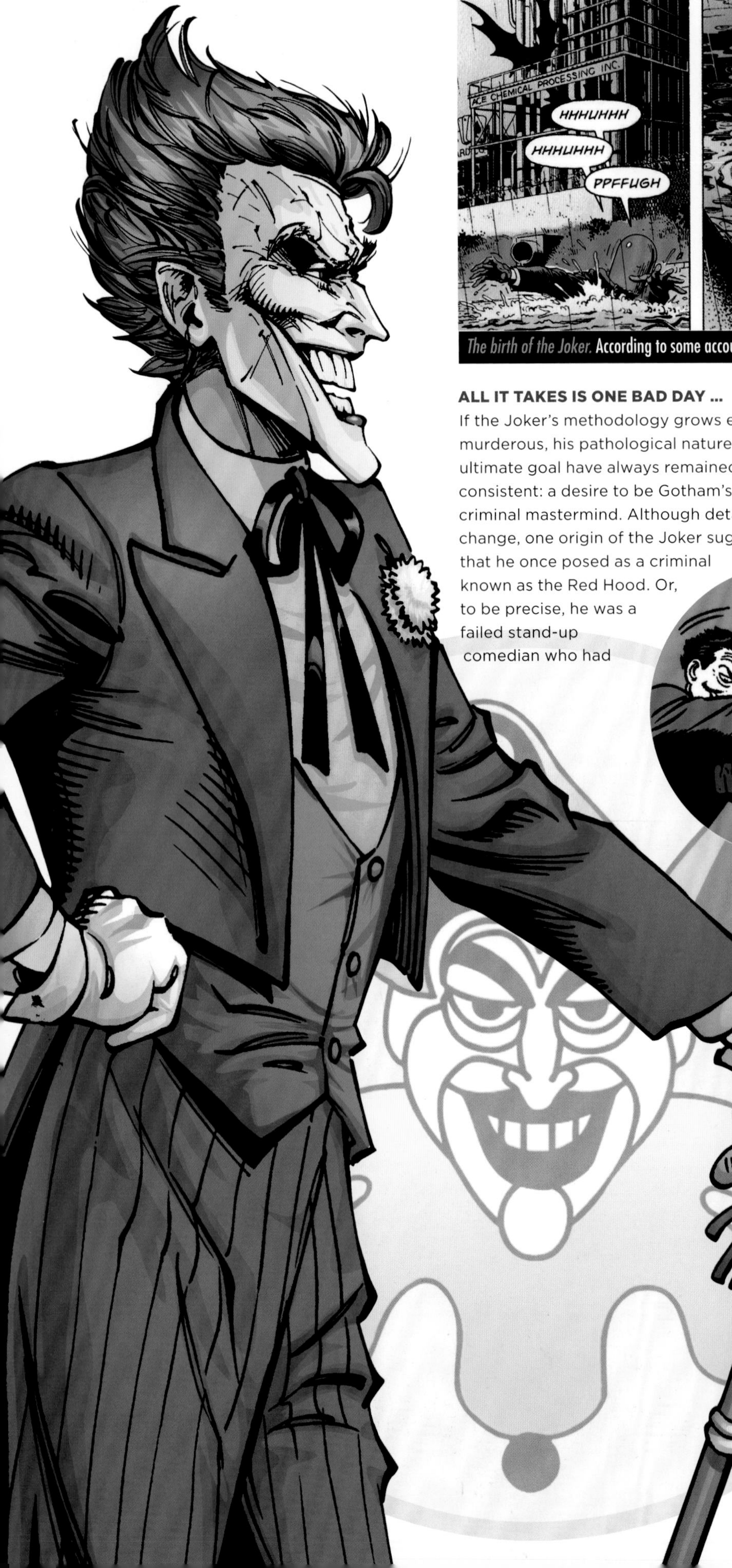

TWISTED MYTHS

Later additions to the origin myth have suggested that the Joker is actually a born sociopath who, as a boy, was exposed to the cruel ministrations of an insane father who physically abused his mother. The boy listened through the wall to her suffering, and enjoyed it in the same way that he derived pleasure from killing small animals. There are other embellishments, but all of these may be obfuscations on the Joker's part, as they're told from his own memories and it's a sound bet that they're deliberately unreliable.

Whatever the precise nature of his beginnings, the Joker's criminal status grew rapidly. With trademark weaponry (cyanide pies, lethal electric hand buzzers, acid sprays, and Joker venom in various forms),

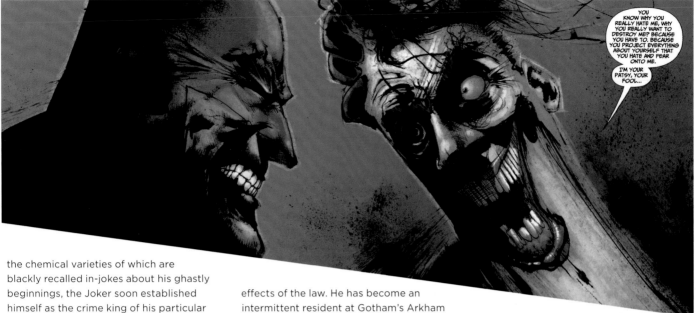

the chemical varieties of which are blackly recalled in-jokes about his ghastly beginnings, the Joker soon established himself as the crime king of his particular domain. There have been many occasions when Batman has been tempted to rid the world of the Joker once and for all, but if the Dark Knight kills the Joker, then that makes him a killer too and, essentially, as evil as his nemesis – and the Joker gets the final victory.

TAKING OVER THE ASYLUM
On the many occasions that the Joker has been caught, he has been declared insane. He may be a serial killer but to a great degree, his status as insane has cushioned him from the effects of the law. He has become an intermittent resident at Gotham's Arkham Asylum for the Criminally Insane – a dangerous situation, for he seems ever to outwit his jailers and psychiatrists, knowing full well how to manipulate them to achieve his own anarchic ends. Arkham itself seems to represent a kind of refuge for the Joker: a place he can go to let off some steam while cultivating his next plan. A remark once attributed to a prominent psychotherapist at Arkham showed a shrewd insight into the Joker's shifting persona: she posited that he possessed some kind of "super-sanity... a brilliant new modification of human perception." The idea behind the theory is that he has no actual personality as he has no control over the sensory information he receives from the outside world. The only way he can cope with the chaotic barrage of input is to create himself a new identity each day. This sheds some light on why he can be merely a mischievous prankster one day and a cold-blooded psychopathic killer the next.

The Joker has, surprisingly, been capable of more "normal" emotions as well: an on-off relationship with former psychiatrist Dr. Harleen Quinzel that certainly got quite heated. This began during one of the Joker's

Crazy in love. The Joker and Harley Quinn – a match made in Arkham Asylum.

stays at Arkham Asylum, when Ms. Quinzel treated him. Unfortunately, she rapidly developed an obsession for her patient. Transformed by the intensity of her desire into the Joker's new sidekick Harley Quinn, she almost succeeded in killing Batman in her quest to win the Joker's love. Their extraordinary relationship is characterized by cruelty heaped upon cruelty, with the Joker often degrading her and sometimes plotting her death. It is, however, occasionally punctuated by what can only be read as moments of real affection, and the mere fact of its existence is the best evidence available that the Joker is actually capable of caring for another human being.

On one occasion, while resident at Slabside Penitentiary (the Slab), the Joker himself was the victim of a practical joke of sorts. When he was discovered to have a brain tumor, a prison doctor modified the Joker's CAT scan so it looked as if his

patient's time was running out. The Joker's reaction was to infect the other inmates with Joker Venom and escape, intending to "Jokerize" the entire world. Evidently, the Joker does have a well-developed sense of his own mortality. His clowning around literally caused worldwide chaos, and the resolution to this particular episode saw his death at the hands of former Robin, Dick Grayson (now Nightwing).

Nightwing's showdown with the Joker was fuelled by a sense of rage that may have been sparked by a moral debate with Barbara Gordon, the former Batgirl, as to whether there can ever be a justification for the act of taking a human life. This time around, Nightwing seemed to think so as he pounded the Joker to death, only to see him resuscitated by Batman, who didn't want his friend to end up with blood on his hands and a murderous act to haunt him for life.

FAMILY MATTERS

Barbara Gordon, perhaps more than any other member of Batman's extended family, could be expected to hold a bitter grudge against the Joker. She was shot and crippled by him, violently ending her career as Batgirl. The Joker wanted to prove to Batman that "all it takes is one bad day to make a normal man go insane," and this was his first move in an attempt to make Jim Gordon, Barbara's father, a kindred spirit. He didn't break the commissioner, of course, but this incident was a foreshadowing of worse to come: Gordon's wife Sarah was shot dead in cold blood by the Joker when she attempted to protect a baby from his twisted scheme.

Batgirl. Barbara Gordon – just one of the Joker's victims.

Interestingly, for once the Joker showed no great pleasure in this act, although in a rare display of tit-for-tat and perhaps understandable revenge, Jim Gordon shot him in the knee. Small recompense, some would say, for crippling his niece and then murdering the woman he loved.

JOKING APART
Others close to Batman have suffered. Nightwing's near-pummeling to death of the Joker uncomfortably echoed an earlier event when his successor Jason

Todd, the second Robin, also fell prey to the malevolent clown. Todd discovered that his birth mother was being blackmailed by the Joker and followed an investigative trail that eventually saw both him and his mother lured to an abandoned warehouse. There he was surprised by the Joker before being mercilessly beaten by his supposed quarry. As Batman arrived on the scene, the Joker blew up the building, along with Todd.

ALWAYS LEAVE 'EM LAUGHING
During one of his extended holidays at Arkham Asylum, the Joker was accused of a set of murders he didn't commit, where the victims were found with his trademark grin after they'd licked some poisoned stamps. The Joker was incensed that something so unimaginative could be attributed to him and declared his innocence in the matter. Batman believed he was telling the truth because the Joker always took credit for his crimes. The Joker was sentenced to death and it was up to the Dark Knight to find the real killer and clear his enemy's name. He succeeded, but the case stretched Batman's devotion to justice to the nth degree.

PUNCHLINE
The Joker then changed tactics yet again. After throwing Commissioner Gordon off a roof, the arch-villain ran amok, but someone dressed as Batman shot the Joker in the face and threw his body in a dumpster. The Joker was reduced to a wheelchair-bound shadow of his former

The Last laugh. The Joker murders Jason Todd, the second Robin.

self, but he was planning a suitably theatrical rebirth. With help from Harley Quinn, he underwent physical therapy – and stitched his own face into a permanent rictus grin. As a typically deranged final touch, he tried to kill Harley – but she was saved by Batman's intervention and shot her 'Puddin'.' After all, he deserved it...

SALVATION RUN
When the US government approved a plan to exile the world's worst supervillains, the Joker was one of the recidivists sent to Cygnus 4019 via Boom Tube. The world turned out to be a planet used for training by the legions of Apokolips. When the mega-powerful psychic, Psimon, nominated himself leader, the Joker proved that superpowers were no match for sheer insanity by beating Psimon's head in with a rock before leading his followers in a war against rival Lex Luthor. The Joker defeated the mastermind in a one-on-one battle, before the villains returned to Earth. The Joker was soon

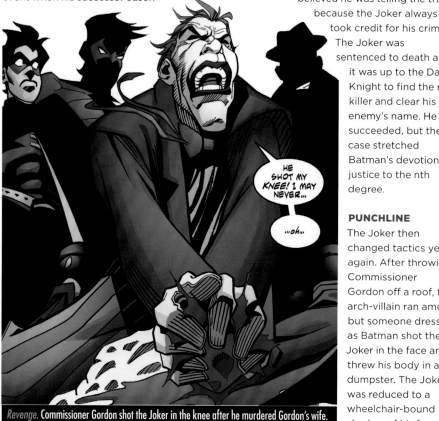

HE SHOT MY KNEE! I MAY NEVER...

...oh...

Revenge. Commissioner Gordon shot the Joker in the knee after he murdered Gordon's wife.

Dumpster. The Batman imposter disposes of the Joker's body.

Cygnus 4019. The Joker and Lex Luthor at each other's throats.

re-imprisoned in Arkham, but the Black Glove conspiracy then attempted to recruit him into their scheme to kill Batman. The Joker claimed that they could not succeed where he had failed – and viciously attacked several of the group. He then escaped Arkham by hijacking an ambulance. The Joker's prediction proved correct – Batman escaped from the coffin the Black Glove had placed him in, and survived a battle in which he killed the group's leader, Dr. Hurt, by crashing his helicopter into the Gotham River.

GRAVE RETURN
Bruce Wayne was presumed killed in action during the *Final Crisis*, and Dick Grayson took on the cowl of Batman. The Joker did not consider Grayson or Damian (the New Robin) worthy adversaries and left town – but when Bruce Wayne returned, so did the Joker. He stole the identity of murderous crime author Oberon Sexton and in this guise he helped Damian Wayne to defeat remaining members of the Black Glove, trying to gain the boy's confidence. However, Damian saw through this ruse and beat him with a crowbar – a brutal reversal of the Joker's slaying of Jason Todd. The Joker then incapacitated Damian with Joker Venom, but the lad was saved by Dick Grayson and the returned Bruce Wayne. Bruce Wayne handed the

role of Batman to Dick Grayson, while he concentrated on setting up the multinational Batman Incorporated franchise. Deprived of the opportunity to torment the 'proper' Batman, the Joker stayed uncharacteristically inactive – until he slaughtered his way out of Arkham, leaving a bloody trail.

Commissioner Gordon's wife was then attacked in her hotel room with Joker Venom, so Batman tracked the Joker down to his hideout in a church crypt. After lashing out at Grayson, mocking him as a 'little bird' and finally begging for his old opponent to come and play with him, the Clown Prince of Crime admitted that the person who had triggered his murder spree (by doctoring his medication) and attacked Mrs. Gordon was none other than her own son, the psychopathic James Jr.

ENFORCED ALLIANCES
The Joker returned to torment the Dark Knight by appearing to cut off the faces of his closest allies, and later by infecting the Justice League – and most of Gotham – with a deadly new toxin (See *The New 52*). He vanished for a while after he – and Batman – apparently died after a battle by the Dionesium pool beneath Gotham. Yet its powers of immortality evidently came into play, as both ultimately returned.

At some point he and Batman were forced to team up as both were targeted by a deadly virus. The search for its origins, , forced them on a bizarre road trip across Europe, ultimately finding that the cure lay in the hands of Bane.

The Joker was later found imprisoned in a hidden room in the Batcave, but escaped to smash a machine invented by the Dark Knight, claiming the device would spell the end of the world. When Batman accidentally unleashed the seven Dark Knights from the Dark Multiverse, one was the insane Batman Who Laughs, driven mad by the Joker of his own reality. The Joker helped Batman defeat the twisted embodiment of both old enemies, along with help from the Justice League, and prevented the Dark God Barbatos from inflicting darkness on our reality.

Although the Joker is a crazed killer beyond compare, his sole reason for existence is to be Batman's lunatic nemesis – and deprived of his caped enemy, he would be but a gibbering shadow of his former self.

Tables turned. Damian attacks the Joker.

THE CLOWN PRINCE

IN THE POST-FLASHPOINT UNIVERSE, THE JOKER IS STILL AN UNHINGED KILLER OBSESSED WITH TORMENTING BATMAN – IF ANYTHING, HE IS EVEN MORE MYSTERIOUS THAN HIS PRE-FLASHPOINT INCARNATION!

Infiltration. Bruce Wayne's undercover disguise is found out by the Red Hood Gang.

No one knows the true origins of the Joker – any attempts by Batman to uncover his nemesis' background have just uncovered more mysteries. Before he became the Joker, he was known as Red Hood One, leader of the terrorist Red Hood Gang – a group made up of prominent citizens who were blackmailed into joining by its boss. Red Hood One appeared to bear a special grudge against the Wayne family and their dedication to building a better Gotham. In his nihilistic worldview, chaos and insanity are inevitable, and all human achievements are ultimately doomed to fall into disorder.

THE FALL OF RED HOOD ONE
When a young Bruce Wayne returned to Gotham following an extended time abroad,

he fought the Red Hood Gang as a vigilante, first infiltrating the group and then foiling their plan to hijack a blimp. Red Hood One took revenge by blowing up Wayne's apartment, beating him, taunting him about the deaths of his parents, and then leaving him to die. However, Bruce survived and took to the streets as Batman for the first time. He tracked the gang to the Ace Chemical Plant, where they were manufacturing a

flesh-dissolving toxin to unleash on Gotham. Batman swooped in, and in an explosive battle Red Hood One plunged into a vat of chemicals and disappeared from sight.

This spelled the end for Red Hood One, but the villain resurfaced as the pale-skinned and maniacal Joker. Over the next five years he committed a series of heinous crimes, including 114 murders, before finally being apprehended and incarcerated in Arkham Asylum. However, this was all part of the Joker's plan. He had psychotic surgeon the Dollmaker skin his face (symbolizing rebirth) before slipping out of Arkham and Gotham. His face was kept on ice in the asylum, and a mob of face-painted Joker fans held a 'vigil' outside in honor of their demented hero.

DEATH OF THE FAMILY
The Joker returned a year later and stole his face from Arkham, stapling it back into place. After murdering 14 GCPD officers and terrifying

Birth of the Joker. Red Hood One falls into a chemical vat.

Tribute for the insane. **The Joker's face in Arkham Asylum.**

Imposter. **Eric Border reveals his true identity to an imprisoned Batman.**

Commissioner Gordon, he unveiled his plans to destroy the entire Batman 'family'. After capturing Batman, he forced him to sit on an electric chair and subjected him to several thousand volts before making him the 'guest of honor' at a dinner in the Batcave. The other guests were the tied-up and face-bandaged Red Robin, Red Hood (Jason Todd), Robin, Nightwing, and Batgirl, and the meal put before them was apparently... their own faces. Batman broke free and released his family members before taking on the Joker

in hand-to-hand combat. During the battle Batman claimed to know the Joker's name, and this terrified the Clown Prince of Crime, who chose to hurl himself into the depths of the Earth rather than hear it.

This appeared to be the end of the Joker, but interest in the theatrical maniac did not abate. Dr. Mahreen Zaheer published a book in which she claimed that the Joker was once Liam Distal, who had suffered terrible abuse in childhood. Arkham orderly Eric Border had helped her in her research – but then revealed that he was actually the Joker in disguise, and told Zaheer that he had been toying with her! The Joker then commenced a reign of terror, first infecting the Justice League with a psychosis-inducing virus and then releasing it in Gotham City, causing the citizens to go mad and attack each other.

Batman raced against time to create a cure, which needed the rare compound dionesium (found in the life-prolonging Lazarus Pits). He sought help from the Court of Owls, who revealed that the highest known concentration of dionesium was in the Joker's blood – and that the being now known as the Joker was alive 400 years ago...

As Batman gathered his 'family' (and many of his villainous enemies) to launch an all-out attack on the Joker to get his blood and save Gotham, he was enacting the latest scene in an eternal drama: the battle between order and the malignant chaos that makes a mockery of human existence – the madness embodied by the Joker!

Family drama. **Batman is fried as the Joker lays on dinner for his captured comrades.**

Reign of terror. **Superman is infected by the Joker's virus.**

THE JOKER FILES

THE GOTHAM CITY POLICE'S CRIME FILES ARE BULGING WITH CASES INVOLVING THE JOKER. HERE ARE JUST A FEW EXAMPLES OF WHY HE IS CONSIDERED ONE OF THE MOST DANGEROUS CRIMINALS AROUND.

GCPD RECORD #JK89636

The Laughing Fish/Sign of the Joker

Only the Joker could come up with such a crazy plan. He dumped chemicals into the sea that gave fish Joker faces and then tried to claim copyright on these mutated fish so he could get royalties. But when Gotham City officials refused the Joker his claim, he had them killed off one by one until his request was granted.

Even with Batman's protection two officials were murdered by the devious Joker's schemes until the Clown Prince of Crime's ego got the better of him and he attempted a killing personally.

Batman was waiting for him and a chase ensued across a construction site in the middle of a thunderstorm. The Joker stepped onto a suspended iron beam just as a bolt of lightning struck and it plunged into a raging river below, never to resurface.

GCPD RECORD #JK43817

Emperor Joker

In possibly his most grandiose scheme ever, the Joker tricked Mr Mxyzptlk into giving him 99.9% of his powers. The fifth-dimensional imp, a constant annoyance to Superman, only intended to give the Joker 1% of his powers because he was bored and "wanted to see what would happen." Instead he unleashed an almost unstoppable force that threatened to destroy the very fabric of time and space.

The Joker began by declaring himself emperor of Earth and remodelled the planet in his own maniacal image, changing many things,

including people's memories. In his world, Superman, Batman and the Justice League were all public enemies, and his own stooges, led by a warped Bizarro Superman, were sent to hunt them down.

Only Superman seemed to realize that something was seriously wrong with reality and, with the help of Steel and Supergirl among others, set out to bring an end to the Joker's reign. This almost impossible task was finally achieved when Superman convinced the Joker that despite all his efforts to erase Batman's presence from his warped universe, he couldn't erase it from his own memory. The Joker retreated back into madness as his powers reverted to Mr Mxyzptlk.

GCPD RECORD #JK15993

No Man's Land

Gotham City had been officially declared a "no man's land" after a series of disasters and was cut off from the outside world by the destruction of bridges and transport links. Those that remained lived under the threat of crime and criminals gone mad. Only Batman and a skeleton police force, led by Commissioner Gordon, were left to try and uphold the law. In the midst of this chaos, the Joker hatched one of his most vile plans yet. He decided to kill all the babies born during the city's lockdown. By distracting Batman, Robin and Nightwing, he very nearly carried out his evil plan, but was stopped at the last moment by Commissioner Gordon's wife, Sarah. In typical Joker fashion he changed his mind and killed her instead of the infants.

When Gordon arrived, just moments too late to save his wife, the Joker gave himself up in the insane hope that, by killing him, Gordon would break the laws he had sworn to keep. Instead the grief-stricken commissioner, rather than extract revenge, shot the Joker in the knee.

GCPD RECORD #JK22458

Gotham Emergency

The Joker felt that his rightful "role" as Gotham City's public enemy number one was under threat. Worried that the press and the city's population were neglecting him, he came up with a deadly scheme to attack both groups by planting explosive devices at a newspaper office and public areas like a baseball stadium and a busy hospital. For good measure he infected the hospital's computer system with a virus that displayed a countdown to each crime.

After two of the devices exploded, Batman finally caught up with the Joker, who during their fight got a face full of his own Smilex venom. Combined with the Joker's mixed-up physiology, the serum put the villain into a critical condition. Batman was forced to save Joker's life in order to find out where the third bomb was located. To this end, he rushed him into the ER of the very hospital where the last bomb was hidden. With the help of the medical staff, the Joker was resuscitated and revealed the location to Batman just in time.

JOKER VENOM

Joker Venom is the Joker's very own patented nerve toxin. Its effects are predictably hideous. Victims are placed into anaphylactic shock caused by blockage of calcium and potassium channels. Facial features contort to resemble Joker's trademark grin. Skin pallor and hair color often change to match Joker's complexion. Depending on the strength of dose and strain of venom used victims are rendered unconscious or, quite literally, die laughing.

The venom is delivered in different ways. Most common is a gaseous form, but it can also be administered as a liquid poison that can be hidden in food or drink or injected by a dart or syringe.

Treatment is possible. Batman has developed an antitoxin that must be given within one hour if the victim is to survive. If left longer, chances of survival are dramatically reduced. However, since the Joker has been known to alter the formula of the venom from time to time, even this cannot be guaranteed.

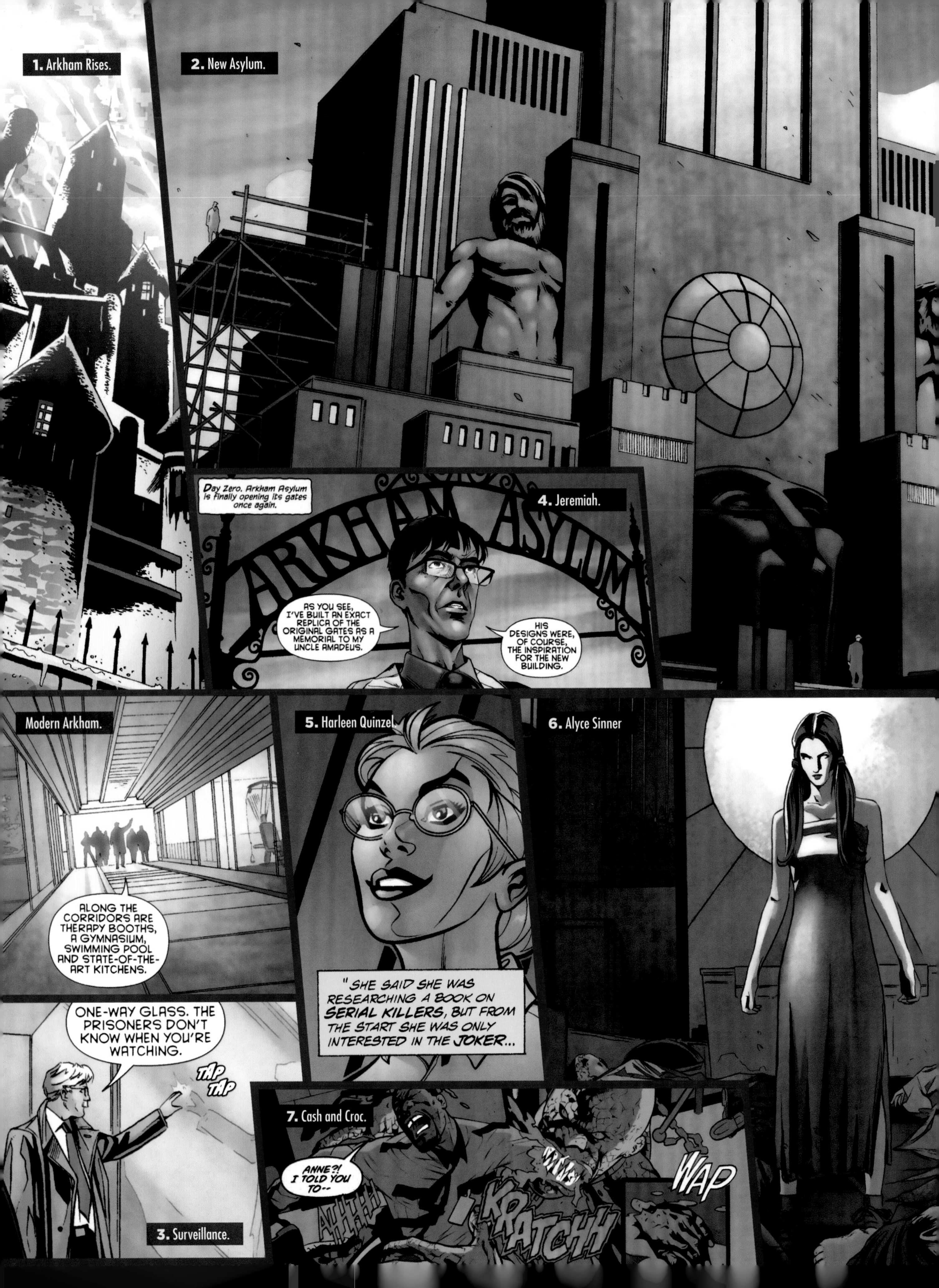
1. Arkham Rises.
2. New Asylum.
Day Zero. Arkham Asylum is finally opening its gates once again.
4. Jeremiah.
ARKHAM ASYLUM
AS YOU SEE, I'VE BUILT AN EXACT REPLICA OF THE ORIGINAL GATES AS A MEMORIAL TO MY UNCLE AMADEUS.
HIS DESIGNS WERE, OF COURSE, THE INSPIRATION FOR THE NEW BUILDING.
Modern Arkham.
ALONG THE CORRIDORS ARE THERAPY BOOTHS, A GYMNASIUM, SWIMMING POOL AND STATE-OF-THE-ART KITCHENS.
ONE-WAY GLASS. THE PRISONERS DON'T KNOW WHEN YOU'RE WATCHING.
TAP TAP
3. Surveillance.
5. Harleen Quinzel.
"SHE SAID SHE WAS RESEARCHING A BOOK ON SERIAL KILLERS, BUT FROM THE START SHE WAS ONLY INTERESTED IN THE JOKER...
6. Alyce Sinner
7. Cash and Croc.
ANNE?! I TOLD YOU TO--
KRATCHH
WAP

ARKHAM ASYLUM

SINCE THE ORIGINAL INSTITUTION OPENED IN 1921, GOTHAM CITY'S HOME FOR THE CRIMINALLY INSANE HAS DEALT WITH SOME OF THE MOST MENTALLY UNHINGED PEOPLE IN THE WORLD AND THERE'S NO SHORTAGE OF NEW PATIENTS.

1. THE FIRST ASYLUM

The original Elizabeth Arkham Asylum for the Criminally Insane had a gruesome history. It was once the family home of Amadeus Arkham. Amadeus's mother, Elizabeth, had suffered mental problems her whole life and apparently committed suicide (although it was later revealed that Amadeus had killed her to end her suffering). Amadeus had worked in Metropolis State Psychiatric Hospital before deciding to transform the family home into a hospital for the mentally disturbed. Shortly before it opened, Amadeus' wife and child were brutally assaulted and killed by Martin "Mad Dog" Hawkins (an ex-patient of Amadeus' from his time in Metropolis). The Asylum still opened as planned; Hawkins was one of its first patients. Amadeus treated him for six months before snapping; in a rage, he electrocuted his wife's killer. This was declared an accident, but the consequences could not be shirked so easily. Amadeus ended up losing his grip on sanity, and he became a patient in his own asylum.

The old Asylum had a terrible record; many inmates escaped, or returned to madness once they left the institution. It was severely damaged several times – most notably when Bane released all the inmates in an attempt to defeat Batman. Eventually, Arkham was moved to a new facility – the renovated, gothic home of the Mercy family. The new facility did little to improve the Asylum's record, which is possibly one of the reasons Batman created a secret Batcave under the establishment. In his attempt to become the new leader of Gotham City's criminals, the Black Mask actually destroyed it in an explosion. In the ruins of the building, Dr. Jeremiah Arkham (the nephew of Arkham's founder) found blueprints created by Amadeus Arkham for a new asylum. He used these to create the present building.

2. THE CURRENT ASYLUM

The new Arkham's gates are a replica of those of the original. The central block of the main building is based on 18th-century English philosopher and social theorist Jeremy Bentham's Panopticon – a prison designed to allow inmates to be constantly observed. Its cells are constructed around a central tower housing the Operations Center. This unit rotates at a rate of one revolution per hour, allowing the Asylum's director to maintain direct visual contact with many of the inmates. Security has been maximized, with cameras operating 24/7 in all cells and areas.

3. TOTAL SURVEILLANCE

The front wall of each cell is made of one-way glass so the inmates can be seen at all times. As an added security measures, each prisoner has a chip in their brain that allows them to be tracked and incapacitated with just a touch of a button, and all exterior windows have heat detectors and microwave motion detectors. The most psychotic inmates have solitary confinement cells, while "normal" patients have a communal dining area. The new Arkham also contains several secret rooms – including a maze under the main building.

4. JEREMIAH ARKHAM

One of the longest serving directors was Jeremiah Arkham. Jeremiah oversaw three versions of the Asylum and countless minor rebuilding programmes. He provided the most accurate description of Arkham and its purpose: "Arkham Asylum is not just any institution for the criminally insane. It's the Ivy League of insanity. A 'Harvard' for psychopaths." Following the revelation that he was in fact the insane criminal and gang boss, the Black Mask, Jeremiah became the latest of Arkham's staff to be committed as a patient.

5. HARLEY QUINN

Many of the directors and psychiatrists working in the hospital have often made their patients look sane. Perhaps the most infamous is Harley Quinn, who, as Harleen Quinzel, studied the Joker while working at Arkham – and fell in love with him.

6. ALYCE SINNER

Jeremiah has been succeeded as director by Dr. Alyce Sinner, his ex-assistant. Alyce harbours a dark secret – she is a mass murderer and a member of Intergang's Church of Crime.

7. AARON CASH

The institute's Corrections Officer Aaron Cash is one of the few people working at Arkham whom Batman respects and trusts. Aaron's hand was bitten off during an incident with Killer Croc. He replaced the hand with a hook, and still bears a grudge against the villain.

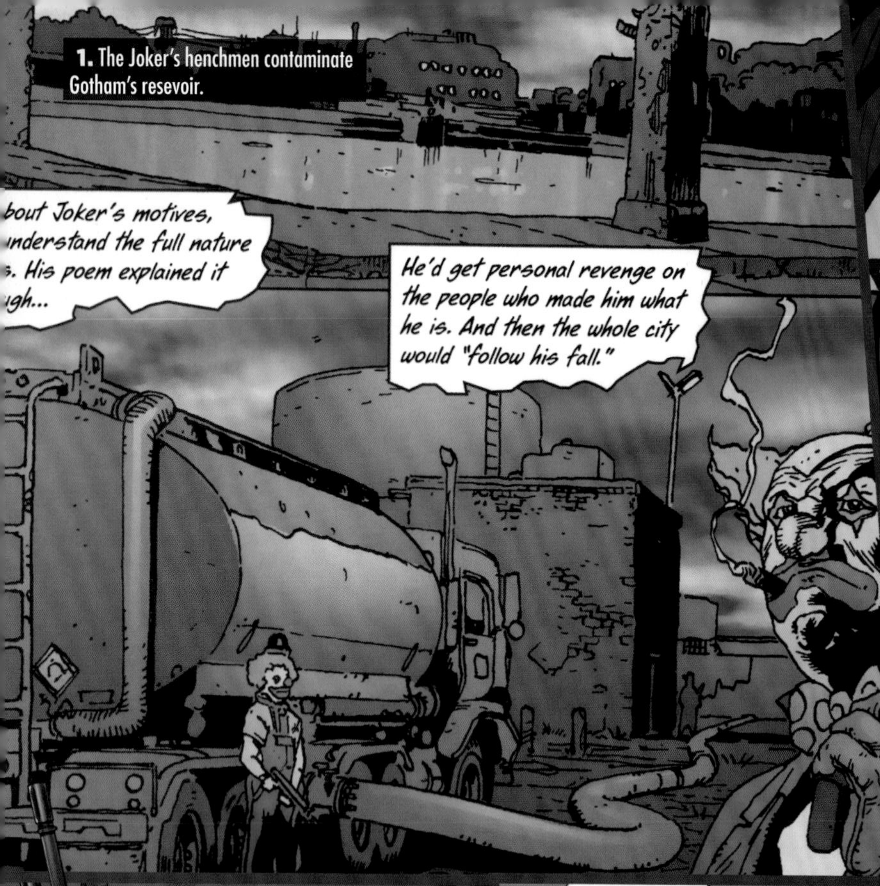
bout Joker's motives,
nderstand the full nature
. His poem explained it
gh...
He'd get personal revenge on the people who made him what he is. And then the whole city would "follow his fall."
1. The Joker's henchmen contaminate Gotham's resevoir.

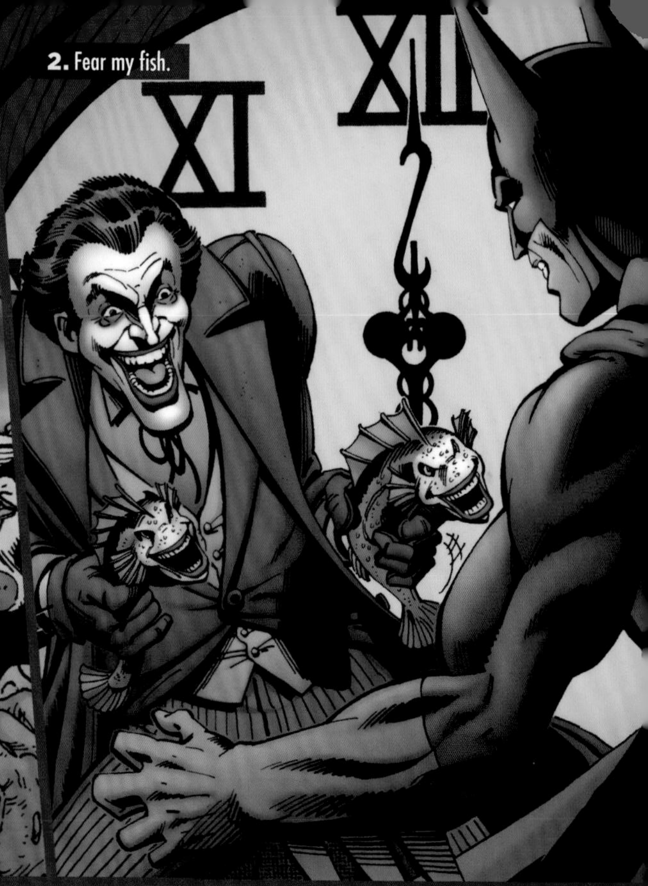
2. Fear my fish.

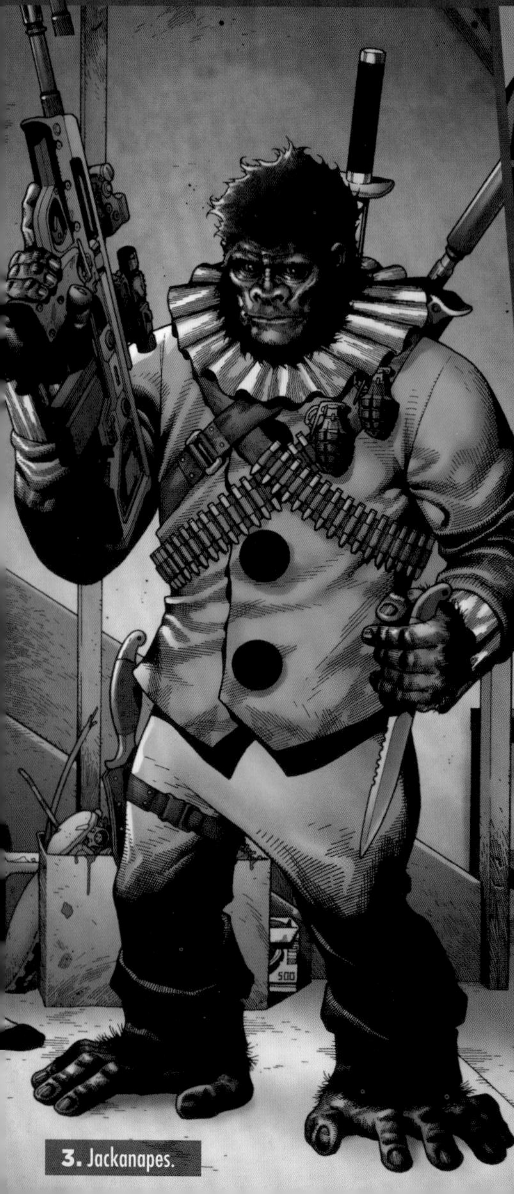
3. Jackanapes.

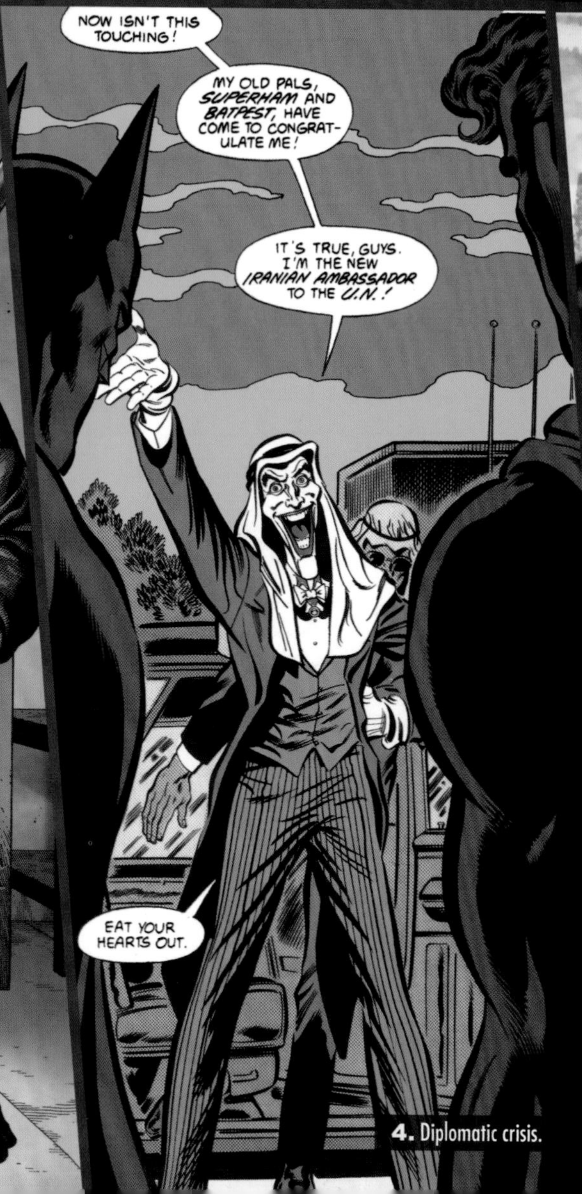
NOW ISN'T THIS TOUCHING!
MY OLD PALS, SUPERHAM AND BATPEST, HAVE COME TO CONGRAT-ULATE ME!
IT'S TRUE, GUYS. I'M THE NEW IRANIAN AMBASSADOR TO THE U.N.!
EAT YOUR HEARTS OUT.
4. Diplomatic crisis.

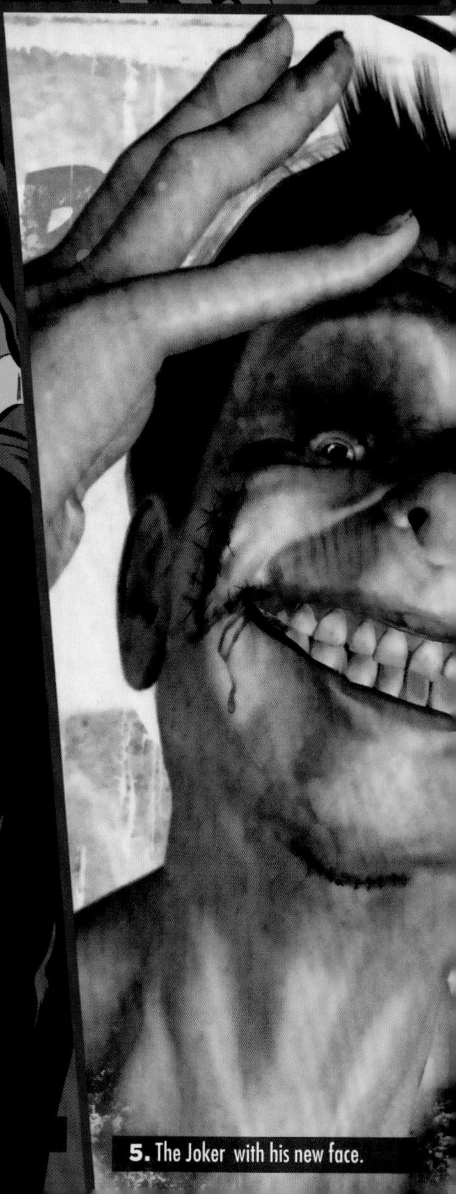
5. The Joker with his new face.

CRAZY CRIMES

THERE IS NO RHYME OR REASON TO THE JOKER'S CRIMINAL ACTS. HE STRIKES WITHOUT WARNING, LEAVING CHAOS AND COUNTLESS VICTIMS IN HIS WAKE. HIS INSANITY MAKES IT IMPOSSIBLE FOR BATMAN AND THE POLICE TO PREDICT HIS ACTIONS.

1. POISONING THE WELL

The Joker's first demented act of criminality was to murder the men he held responsible for his descent into madness. He confounded both Batman and the police to poison the board members of the Ace Chemicals Processing Company. Such a small act of vengeance wasn't grand enough for the Clown Prince of Crime, however, and he planned to make everyone suffer for his plight. He contaminated the Old Gotham Reservoir with his Joker venom, hoping to ensure that the entire city died with a leering grin on its face. Batman ultimately foiled the villain's plan – but the Grand Guignol tone of the Joker's murderous schemes was well and truly established.

2. LAUGHING FISH

The Joker's most audacious use of his deadly venom was when he used the toxic brew to contaminate Gotham City's fish supply. The entire catch developed leering grins, identical to the Joker's own malign smile. Because he owned the copyright to his own image, the Joker hoped to rake in millions in royalties. The copyright commission didn't see it that way, though, even after the Joker started bumping off its members. Perhaps inevitably, Batman became the ultimate arbiter in the bizarre trademark dispute. The arch foes battled during a fearsome thunderstorm... and a bolt of lightning struck the Joker. He plunged into the waters of Gotham Bay and, for a time, it was believed that the villain was finally "sleeping with the fishes."

3. MONKEY BUSINESS

Reminded of a soft toy that he cherished as a child, the Joker absconded from Gotham City Zoo with a baby gorilla. He called his new companion Jackanapes, dressing him in a clown suit and arming him with machine guns and grenades. They were seemingly inseparable partners-in-crime for some considerable time – at least in the Joker's demented mind. Learning that the city planned to demolish the zoo, the Joker led Jackanapes in an assault on the council chambers. The villain used radical sound waves to transform the councillors into brain-dead zombies. In the ensuing fight, Jackanapes was killed... but with the council in disarray the zoo was saved!

4. MURDER MOST FOUL

First he bludgeoned him with a crowbar, then he blew him up. The manner in which the Joker dispatched Robin (aka Jason Todd) was cold and very, very calculating. It was designed to cause the Dark Knight the most anguish – to drive the hero to the edge of madness with grief. In the immediate aftermath of Jason's death, the Joker took a role with the Iranian government, but if he thought his newly acquired diplomatic immunity would save him from Batman's wrath, he was sorely mistaken. The Dark Knight planned to take down the Joker once and for all – at least he did until warned off by the US government and Superman. In the end, though, the Joker over-played his hand, attacking the UN General Assembly and giving both Batman and the Man of Steel a legitimate reason to act.

5. BATTLE SCARS

After being shot in the head by a deranged police officer, the Joker underwent intensive reconstructive surgery. The doctors did their best to restore his shattered face, but he was left with a permanent grin – unable to move his mouth at all. The Joker's even ghastlier new appearance brought about a spiritual rebirth. He was transformed from the Clown of Crime into the Clown Prince of Cruelty. To celebrate his metamorphosis, he dispatched Harley Quinn to kill all his previous henchmen. The denouement of the Joker's demented scheme was to be the murder of Harley Quinn on the steps of Arkham Asylum. An intervention from Batman saved Harley, but she was left wondering about the Joker's motives. "Don'tcha love me no more?" was her plaintive cry.

A cinema-length animated movie of Batman: **The Killing Joke** was released in 2016 with all-new scenes added to the story.

BATMAN: THE KILLING JOKE

MARCH 1988

THIS IS REGARDED as one of the greatest graphic novels of all time. Writer Alan Moore and artist Brian Bolland created a tense and controversial tale which juxtaposes a possible origin of the Joker with his attempt to drive Commissioner Gordon insane. The Joker has never appeared so terrifying, so without compassion, as when he puts Gordon through physical and emotional torture in an attempt to break the commissioner's mind, and shoots Barbara Gordon at point-blank range. Bolland's image of the Joker cackling wildly, moments after his transformation into the pale-faced, leering villain we know, has become one of the most iconic images of the Clown Prince of Crime, influencing many later artists.

A DEATH IN THE FAMILY

(BATMAN #426-429)
DECEMBER 1988-JANUARY 1989

ONE OF THE MOST NOTORIOUS STORIES in Batman's history, "A Death in the Family", by Jim Starlin and Jim Aparo, told of the new Robin (Jason Todd)'s search for his birth mother in parallel with the Joker's attempt to sell a nuclear weapon to Middle Eastern terrorists. Robin's mother turned out to be an embezzler, blackmailed by the Joker into handing over her son. The Joker proceeded to use a crowbar to beat Robin to within an inch of his life. Readers were offered a phone vote to decide the fate of Batman's sidekick. The poll was close, with fewer than 100 votes forcing the outcome – Jason died in an explosion from a bomb set by the Joker.

The tale was part of a new wave of comics dealing with more sophisticated themes aimed at mature readers, with heroes conflicted about how to deal with their enemies. Though death and rebirth was common in comic books, the passing of Jason Todd was a milestone in the narrative of the Dark Knight.

An alternative ending to **Batman #428**, in which Robin survived the bomb, was finally revealed in 2006's **Batman** Annual #25.

ENDGAME

(*BATMAN* VOL.2 #35-40)
DECEMBER 2014-MAY 2015

2011'S DC COMICS: THE NEW 52 introduced a new version of the Harlequin of Hate, insane enough to wear his removed face as a mask. When he returned in "Endgame," the Joker had both a healed face and knowledge of Batman's alter ego, Bruce Wayne. Using an airborne pathogen, he turned Gotham City's citizens into violent copies of himself, and it seemed the only antidote was in the Joker's spinal fluid. As the story ended, in a collapsing cave, Batman and the Joker fought the bloodiest of battles, one that neither combatant seemed likely to survive.

The tale, by the regular *Batman* team of Scott Snyder and Greg Capullo, added even greater depth to the Joker's relationship with Batman, with a potentially unkillable villain tempting a fatally wounded Batman with immortality before the pair faced the ultimate fate side by side.

In this tale, the Dark Knight had to confront the possibility that his arch-nemesis might be a Gotham City immortal called the Pale Man.

THE JOKER

ABOVE ALL OF THE BATMAN'S FOES, IT IS THE JOKER WHO IS HIS ARCHEST OF ENEMIES.

A MASTER CRIMINAL to match a master detective, the leering jester is nothing without a Dark Knight to plot against. His overall aim is the humiliation of Gotham's City's defender.

Initially invented as a throwaway, playing card-inspired gangster with a macabre enjoyment of leaving victims in a grotesque death grin, the Joker was fated to die in his second appearance. But a forward-thinking comic-book editor spotted something special in this pale-faced felon and demanded he return. And return he would, many times, becoming less of a serial killer and more of a comedy-themed criminal. The Joker was keen to announce his audacious plans through radio or newspapers, to taunt the police and, of course, Batman.

Returning to his more murderous roots in the Seventies, the Joker proved his cruel credentials by beating Robin the Boy Wonder to a pulp and leaving him to die in an explosion. He later shot and paralyzed Commissioner Gordon's daughter and murdered his wife. His recent incarnation has proved equally sinister, striking at the Batman's extended 'family' of allies to break the Dark Knight's will. Throughout, the true identity of the Joker has remained a mystery. Was he a failed stand-up comedian? An immortal? A street thug? Or, indeed, more than one of these. The punchline remains to be told.

GOLDEN AGE

A MASTER CRIMINAL LEAVING VICTIMS WEARING A GHASTLY GRIN... THE JOKER PLAYS HIS CARDS.

THE FIRST ISSUE of Batman's own title introduced a grinning serial killer and jewel thief eager to match his wits against Gotham City's finest. Though nothing is said of his origin, his calling card and grin-inducing venom are already in play, along with a lab below a graveyard.

The Joker was the villain in two stories in this first issue. Stabbed by his own hand, he almost met his maker, but in the last panel he survived to haunt Batman and Robin nine times over in the first 12 issues of *Batman*.

The Joker's trail of grinning death was gradually replaced with a series of pranks, as the evildoer found humor in humiliating the Dark Knight. More nuisance than threat, the Joker concocted evermore elaborate schemes, committing backwards, sound-effect and Rebus-themed crimes, utilizing a giant pinball game (*Batman* #44), costumes (*Batman* #63) and a giant vacuum cleaner (*Batman* #136).

In *Detective Comics* #168, Batman's investigation into an old crime led to the revelation that the Joker had a previous identity, the Red Hood. He plotted to steal a million dollars from the Monarch Card Company before escaping through a chemical bath, which gave him his distinctive look with pale skin and green hair. Perhaps the villain had a reliable origin at last...

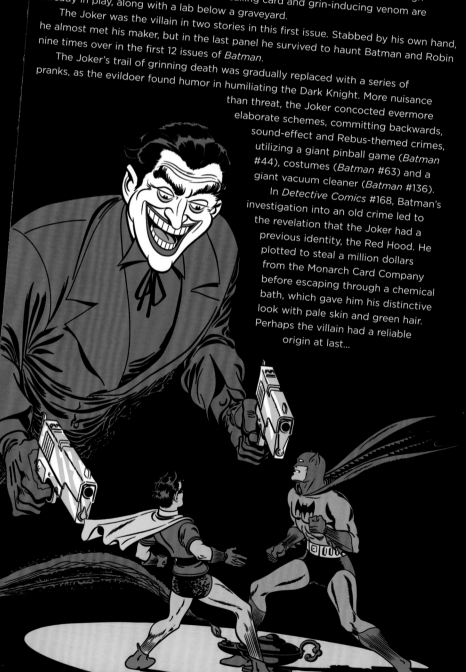

VENOM
leaves the Joker's victims grinning
in *Batman* #1 (Spring 1940)

COVER STAR
The Joker's first cover appearance,
Detective Comics #62 (April 1942)

ELECTRIC CHAIR
The Joker faces execution
in *Detective Comics* #64 (June 1942)

JOKERMOBILE
and JOKER GYRO in *Batman* #37 (November 1946)

RED HOOD
A possible origin for the Joker
in *Detective Comics* #168 (February 1951)

TEAM-UP
The first Lex Luthor/Joker partnership, in
World's Finest #88 (June 1957)

SON
Alfred imagines Batman II (Dick Grayson)
vs the Joker's 'son' in *Batman* #145 (February 1962)

SILVER AGE

THE JOKER'S SIXTIES WERE AS MADCAP AS THE PREVIOUS DECADES, WITH COMEDY-THEMED CRIMES THAT OFFERED MORE MIRTH THAN MENACE.

FBI

The Joker is inducted into the Federation of Bizarro Idiots in *World's Finest* #156 (March 1966)

BULKED UP

The Dark Knight becomes super-sized thanks to the Joker's gas in *Brave and the Bold* #68 (November 1966)

GAGGY

the Joker's one-off sidekick debuts in *Batman* #186 (November 1966)

99¢

for 5 Joker T-shirts undercut Batman's range, *Detective Comics* #365 (July 1967)

LUNATIC

The Joker's moon-themed crimes in *Detective Comics* #388 (June 1969)

WHILE THE JOKER was popularized by Cesar Romero in the Classic TV series in the late Sixties, the character became less of a feature in the comic books. However, his activities had much in common with his television portrayal. His first appearances after Batman got a new look in 1964 saw the Joker committing comedy crimes based on gags and slapstick movies. This included crossing the road on a giant chicken to rob a jewellers while the staff were doubled up with mirth (*Detective Comics* #332) and robbing a bank dressed as Charlie Chaplin (*Detective Comics* #341). The Joker was a nuisance rather than a serious threat and, more often than not, ended each appearance behind bars.

The Joker wasn't averse to allying himself with fellow criminals, siding with both Bizarro Superman and Batman, and Lex Luthor against the World's Finest team-up of Batman and Superman. He also took on a short sidekick, Gaggy, for one caper. The villain revealed a jealous streak too, undercutting a Batman range to sell his own merchandise and profiting from his own pay-TV channel (*Detective Comics* #365).

BRONZE AGE

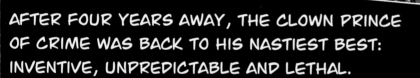

AFTER FOUR YEARS AWAY, THE CLOWN PRINCE OF CRIME WAS BACK TO HIS NASTIEST BEST: INVENTIVE, UNPREDICTABLE AND LETHAL.

THE JOKER'S BRONZE AGE RETURN revived the original menace, dispensing with oversized sets and themed crimes for more wicked schemes that amused his dark insanity.

Having escaped from the State Hospital for the Criminally Insane, the Joker was once again using his signature Joker Venom, leaving victims dying with a grimace, while his exploding cigars included nitro-glycerin. The Joker was a killer, yet when it came to having Batman unconscious at his mercy, he preferred to continue playing "the game," with a wide-awake Dark Knight as his captive audience. The Joker's dark sense of humour led him to shrink his own "shrink" during an escape from Arkham Asylum (*Batman* #286) which seemed to offer a revolving door to its infamous patient.

A memorable plot had the Joker contaminate fish so they all bore his maniacal grin. Then he tried to copyright the result. As he had in his earliest appearances, the Joker also took to pre-announcing his crimes on national television, goading the Dark Knight into action. He had a penchant for strapping Batman to explosive devices rather than facing him with his fists – it appealed to his sense of spectacle. For the Joker, the show would go on!

REVENGE
The Joker returns to Gotham City in *Batman* #251 (September 1973)

ARKHAM
has the Joker as an inmate in *Batman* #258 (October 1974)

9
The Joker gets his own title for nine issues at least (May 1975)

JOKER-FISH
© The Joker, *Detective Comics* #475 (March 1978)

HA-HACIENDA
The Joker's secret base, in a cemetery, *Detective Comics* #476 (April 1978)

500
The Joker leads an army of Batman's enemies in the anniversary *Detective Comics* #526 (May 1983)

JOKER-LAND
The Joker plans to rule Guatamala, following a coup in *Detective Comics* #532 (November 1978)

KILLING JOKE
Is this the origin of the Joker? (March 1988)

JASON TODD
Robin II is killed by the Joker
in *Batman* #428 (February 1989)

HARLEY
The Joker finds his female match
in *Batman: Harley Quinn* #1 (October 1999)

NO MAN'S LAND
The Joker murders Sarah Essen-Gordon
in *Detective Comics* #741 (February 2000)

EMPEROR
The Joker alters reality
in *Superman* Vol. 2 #160 (September 2000)

FACE
The Joker leaves his face behind
in *Detective Comics Vol.2* #1 (November 2001)

DIONESIUM
The secret to the Joker's recovery
Batman #40 (April 2015)

MODERN AGE

BATMAN'S ALLIES BECAME TARGETS AS THE JOKER GAINED A NEW ADMIRER AND CHOSE A GRUESOME NEW LOOK.

1988 WAS A MAJOR YEAR for the Joker, with a definitive take on his origin and some of his most shocking deeds taking place. *Batman: The Killing Joke* saw the threads of the Joker's previous origin tales brought together. In this version, a failed comedian was compelled to commit a burglary to help his pregnant wife. Disguised as the Red Hood, he fell into a vat of chemicals and was turned into a pale, green-haired maniac, driven insane by the transformation and news of his wife's accidental death.

While this origin unwound, the contemporary Clown Prince of Crime showed a stone-hearted cruelty by shooting and paralysing Barbara (Batgirl) Gordon and mentally torturing her father, Commissioner James Gordon. This same disregard for others manifested in the four-part 'A Death in the Family' saga which saw the Joker attempting to sell a cruise missile in the Middle East, and also his well-documented ending of the career of second Robin (Jason Todd).

At the end of the multipart saga 'No Man's Land', the Joker cold-bloodedly shot and killed Gordon's second wife Sarah. The murder failed to raise a smile on the Joker,

The Joker keeps his true identity a closely guarded secret.

With one deliberate shot, The Joker paralyzes Barbara Gordon.

DC COMICS: THE
NEW 52

Following the events of Flashpoint, the Joker ordered the Dollmaker to cut his face off, and he then wore it as a macabre mask. When he returned, it was to strike at Batman's extended family of allies. Next appearing fully healed, with his face intact, and knowing Batman's secret identity, the Joker teased Batman with the possibility that he was an immortal, Gotham City's "Pale Man." The source of his longevity and survival was found to be a pool of Dionesium in the caves below Gotham City. A bloody final battle saw the perennial foes face death. But, months later, both arose with little memory of the past and a future as mutual enemies assured.

The Joker chose to wear his own sliced-off face as a ghoulish mask.

and he gave himself up. Instead of killing the Joker, Gordon shot him in the kneecap, leaving him to jest that it was a fitting revenge for his maiming of Barbara.

While the Joker's cruel nature took center stage, it did nothing to diminish his appeal for his former psychiatrist-turned-lover Harley Quinn. Their relationship was tumultuous to say the least, with both attempting to murder the other.

The Joker's twisted world view came to the fore when he stole the powers of the interdimensional imp Mr. Mxyzptlk and made himself emperor of a world in which Batman died daily. Despite his near omnipotence, the Joker could not quite bring himself to obliterate the Dark Knight forever. A later attempt to rehabilitate the Joker by convincing him he had terminal cancer failed when he launched a 'final' crime spree with an army of Jokerized villains.

The Joker continues his deadly dance with his heroic rival, Batman.

CREDITS

GENERAL EDITOR Ben Robinson

PROJECT MANAGER Jo Bourne

VOLUME EDITORS Jo Bourne, Glenn Dakin, and Richard Jackson

WRITERS Nick Abadzis, Neal Bailey, Alan Cowsill, Glenn Dakin, and Will Potter

COVER DESIGNER Stephen Scanlan

DESIGNERS Katy Everett, Gary Gilbert, James King, Terry Sambridge, and Stephen Scanlan

PACKAGING DESIGNER James King

SUB EDITOR Alice Peebles

COVER ART Jim Lee and Andy Kubert

BATMAN created by Bob Kane with Bill Finger

EAGL41657

Published by Hero Collector Books, a division of Eaglemoss Ltd. 2019

Material originally published by Eaglemoss in: *DC Super Hero Collection* 2008, *DC Chess Collection* 2012, BATMAN UNIVERSE *Collector's Busts* 2018

ISBN 978-1-85875-543-4

Printed in China

THANKS TO:

PENCILERS Neal Adams, Christian Alamy, Rafael Albuquerque, Brent Anderson, Jim Aparo, Ramon Bachs, Mark Bagley, Eddy Barrows, Eric Battle, Ed Benes, Lee Bermejo, Brian Bolland, Brett Booth, Rick Burchett, Chris Burnham, Jim Calafiore, Greg Capullo, Nick Cardy, Sergio Cariello, Sean Chen, Ernie Chua, Andy Clarke, Denys Cowan, Fernando Dagnino, Tony S. Daniel, Shane Davis, Mike DeCarlo, Mike Deodato, Terry Dodson, Dale Eaglesham, Jason Fabok, David Finch, Lee Garbett, Joe Giella, Keith Giffen, Patrick Gleason, Ig Guara, Sam Kieth, Cully Hamner, Jeremy Haun, Clayton Henry, Adam Hughes, Carmine Infantino, Frazer Irving, Klaus Janson, Jock, J.G. Jones, Kelley Jones, Dan Jurgens, Bob Kane, Leonard Kirk, Barry Kitson, Don Kramer, Andy Kubert, Michael Lark, Ken Lashley, Jim Lee, Scott McDaniel, Ed McGuiness, Dave McKean, Doug Mahnke, David Mazzucchelli, Jesús Merino, Mike Mignola, Frank Miller, Sheldon Moldoff, Dustin Nguyen, Ben Oliver, Ariel Olivetti, Diego Olmos, Carlos Pacheco, Fernando Pasarin, Yanick Paquette, Whilce Portacio, Frank Quitely, Ivan Reis, Cliff Richards, Jerry Robinson, Marshall Rogers, Stephane Roux, Jesus Saiz, Tim Sale, Daniel Sampere, Alex Sánchez, Lew Sayre Schwartz, Bart Sears, Damion Scott, Nicola Scott, Walt Simonson, Paulo Siqueira, Ryan Sook, Dick Sprang, Cameron Stewart, Marcus To, John Van Fleet, Bob Wiacek, J.H. Williams III, Pete Woods, Patrick Zirche

INKERS Rafael Albuquerque, Marlo Alquiza, Terry Austin, Ed Benes, Bennett and Jose, Brian Bolland, Chris Burnham, Sal Buscema, Keith Champagne, Vincente Cifuentes, Andy Clarke, Vince Colletta, Scott Daniels, Dan Davis, Mike DeCarlo, Jesse Delperdang, Tom Derenick, Rachel Dodson, Wayne Faucher, Sandu Florea, John Floyd, Derek Fridolfs, Stefano Gaudiano, Dick Giordano, Jonathan Glapion, Jamie Grant, Mick Gray, Wayne Faucher, Eber Ferreira, Sandu Florea, John Floyd, Richard Friend, Scott Hanna, Jeremy Haun, Clayton Henry, Sandra Hope, Rob Hunter, Brian Hurtt, Frazer Irving, Klaus Jansen, Jock, J.G. Jones, Bob Kane, Sam Kieth, Andy Kubert, Michael Lacombe, Mark Lipka, Jay Leisten, Dave McKean, Doug Mahnke, Jason Masters, David Mazzucchelli, Danny Miki, Sheldon Moldoff, Mark Morales, Tom Nguyen, Ariel Olivetti, Diego Olmos, Andy Owens, Jimmy Palmiotti, Charles Paris, Sean Parsons, Mark Pennington, Andrew Pepoy, Joe Prado, Norm Rapmund, Rodney Ramos, Robin Riggs, Jerry Robinson, Alex Ross, George Roussos, Marco Rudy, Greg Scott, Trevor Scott, Tim Sale, Bart Sears, Cam Smith, Dick Sprang, Chris Sprouse, John Stanisci, Lary Stucker, Art Thibert, Wade von Grawbadger, Bob Wiacek, Scott Williams, Ryan Winn, Walden Wong

COLORISTS Christopher Chuckry, Nathan Fairbairn, Jonathan Glapion, Ian Hannin, John Higgins, Matt Hollingsworth, Dave McCaig, Guy Major, Richmond Lewis, Tomeu Morey, Glynis Oliver, Pete Pantazis, FCO Plascencia, Adrienne Roy, Jerry Serpe, Buzz Setzer, Alex Sinclair, Peter Steigerwald, Dave Stewart, John Van Fleet, Lynn Varley

WRITERS Brian Azzarello, Scott Beatty, Ed Brubaker, Eddie Campbell, Tony S. Daniel, Chuck Dixon, Steve Englehart, Bill Finger, Adam Glass, Devlin Grayson, David Hine, Gregg Hurwitz, Geoff Johns, Karl Kesel, Andy Kubert, Jeph Loeb, Sam Kieth, David Mazzucchelli, Frank Miller, Alan Moore, Grant Morrison, Denny O'Neil, Frank Robbins, James Robinson, Greg Rucka, Dan Slott, Jim Starlin, Scott Snyder, Peter J. Tomasi, Len Wein, Judd Winick, Ryan Winn, Daren White